THE FATHERS OF THE EARLY CHURCH

An Adult Resource Book

Willard W. Wetzel, Editor

UNITED CHURCH PRESS
Boston/Philadelphia

Contents

41368

Introduction

THE CHRISTIAN CHURCH had an unpromising beginning in a fascinating "one world" in which political power was centered in Rome and "culture" was Greek. As Paul and Barnabas sailed the Mediterranean, the Roman Empire was approaching the height of its prestige and power. The lands circling the Mediterranean Sea had long been under Roman rule. Now, Roman soldiers were subduing Britain in the northwest, and Roman governors were extending their authority in Syria and in the other states in the east. From the border of Scotland, along the line of the Rhine and the Danube, to the banks of the Euphrates, Roman legions kept watch over the peace and security of the worldwide empire of the Caesars.

The Romans are to be remembered as political geniuses who had an inclination for that which is practical. While they knew nothing about the germ theory of disease, they appreciated the importance of an adequate supply of fresh water for their cities. Whereas they spent little time and effort in the pursuit of the arts, they did provide their world with towering aqueducts, dignified civic buildings, great amphitheaters, and a vast network of "superhighways" and waterways that linked town with town all the way from Jerusalem to London, from Gibraltar to the Black Sea.

After a political power struggle that led to the murder of Julius Caesar in 44 B.C., the Romans moved into strong political structures that were to give rise to worldwide power and success. "Caesar" became one of the titles that was bestowed upon the emperor, along with other titles that would be added at a later date. During the reign of Octavian (27 B.C.–A.D. 14), the senate conferred upon him the title Augustus—meaning majestic. Accordingly, when the biblical record contains the statement, "In those days a decree went out from Caesar Augustus that all the world should be enrolled" (Luke

2:1), the reference is to the Emperor Octavian. Both Caesar and Augustus are titles. Similarly, in Luke 3:1, "Tiberius Caesar" is a reference to the Emperor Tiberius, who ruled from A.D. 14 to A.D. 37.

On the other hand, the fact that the New Testament was written in Greek was not an accident; rather, it is an indication of the way in which the Romans—though they restored law and order to the world and built an empire—enthusiastically adopted the philosophy, the literature, and the art of the conquered Greeks. That their adoption was exceedingly wise is attested to by the Greek genius for theoretical thought, mental speculation, and a sensitivity to beauty expressed in majestic works of art. While the Greek city-states would not unite in a lasting union that alone could have preserved Greece from outside invasion, the Greek climate of freedom and originality was a forerunner of modern democracy. And the Hellenistic influence gave the Roman world a language common to all.

Thus the Roman and the Greek civilizations were complementary, and it is accurate and helpful to think of the world into which Christianity was born as the Greco-Roman world.

Incredible Change in Three Centuries

In the beginning of its life the Christian church was hardly more than a family affair that made little difference in the ongoing life of the Greco-Roman world. The followers of Jesus remained near home and waited for the early return of their Messiah. "Truly, I say to you, you will not have gone through all the towns of Israel, before the Son of man comes" (Matthew 10:23). The book of the Acts of the Apostles pictures James, the brother of Jesus, as the first leader in Jerusalem; and one early history says that a cousin of Jesus became James' successor.

When the early return of Jesus failed to materialize, however, his followers had to come to grips with the world in which they were living. Even so, there was little evidence that the fellowship could be expected to divert the course of world affairs or leave a mark on succeeding generations.

Ironically, though, in three centuries the mighty Roman Empire itself was to become officially Christian. The Christian church was to spread throughout the "world." In these early centuries, the term "catholic" was in common usage to mean general or universal. It frequently appeared in the writings of pagans such as Zeno and

Detail from hundred-foot marble column of Trajan (Roman emperor from A.D. 98–117), erected in Rome during his lifetime. The column commemorates the Roman sweep across the Danube in conquest of the barbarian tribes of Dacia. Such conquests prepared the Greco-Roman world for the spread of Christianity through Europe. The lower section shows Trajan being offered the heads of Dacians by his victorious troops.

3

Polybius. By the second century, Ignatius' letter to Smyrna was to apply the term to the Christian church. Of the Christian fellowship, Cyril of Jerusalem could write that it was denominated Catholic because it was spread from one end of the world to the other.

Out of Efforts at Extermination

This book focuses upon men who were prominent in the experiences of the Christian fellowship in these first three centuries. The book gives summaries of the writings of each of the early church fathers dealt with; and it provides some historical context, including relevant information about the lives of the writers.* It points up those issues dealt with in the writings that are relevant today. It does not discuss the implications of the writings for today; rather, it deals with the issues in their historical settings. Consideration of the issues for our day is left up to the reader or to a study group, especially in light of the fact that no one can adequately tell another person how issues relate to his own present circumstances.

One aspect of the circumstances and experiences of the church fathers of the first three centuries is of great importance in preparation for an excursion into the body of this book. We refer to the fact that these early centuries were by no means lived in a Greco-Roman world congenial to Christianity. Quite the contrary! Much of the life of the early Christians was marked by murderous persecution and by determined efforts toward their extermination.

Probably the story of persecution and efforts at extermination must begin with reference to a playboy Roman emperor, Nero. An ancient writer has provided us with a vivid word picture:

> Nero set up as culprits and punished with utmost refinement of cruelty a class hated for their abominations, who are commonly called Christians. Christus, from whom their name is derived, was executed at the hands of the procurator Pontius Pilate, in the reign of Tiberius. . . . Besides being put to death they were made to serve as objects of amusement; they were clad in hides of beasts and torn to death by dogs; others were crucified.[1]

Peter and Paul apparently paid for their faith with their lives dur-

---

* These summaries are based on information supplied by Jaroslav Jan Pelikan, Titus Street Professor of Ecclesiastical History, Yale University. Original translations of quotations from the early church fathers have been supplied by Dr. Pelikan, except where otherwise noted.

ing the persecutions under Nero, who was emperor from A.D. 54 to A.D. 68. Domitian (81–96), Decius (249–251), Valerian (253–260), Gallienus (253–268), and Diocletian (284–305) are all remembered as having reigned during times of persecution, some periods being more severe than others. Decius issued the edict of A.D. 250, which instigated the first universal and systematic persecution, aimed at extermination. Diocletian instituted the last sustained effort.

The tide turned abruptly in the fourth century. In 311, Galerius promulgated an edict of toleration. Constantine (324–337) issued a declaration of religious freedom for Christians, as he himself accepted their faith.

One cannot help but wonder whether it was a mere coincidence that the Christian church emerged as a world-shaking power at the same time at which it was so bitterly persecuted that there were— at times—determined efforts at its extermination. At any rate, the men whose writings and lives are highlighted in this book lived through such experiences in the fascinating, often hostile, yet always powerful Greco-Roman world.

KUNSTHISTORISCHES MUSEUM, VIENNA

The GEM OF AUGUSTUS, *a first-century onyx cameo depicting the Roman Emperor Augustus* (*Caesar Augustus, 27* B.C.–A.D. *14*) *being crowned king of the world. Victory is holding a wreath over his head, and the Roman eagle is under his chair. Leaving the chariot is Tiberius. The lower section depicts the erection of a Roman standard over fallen captives.*

5

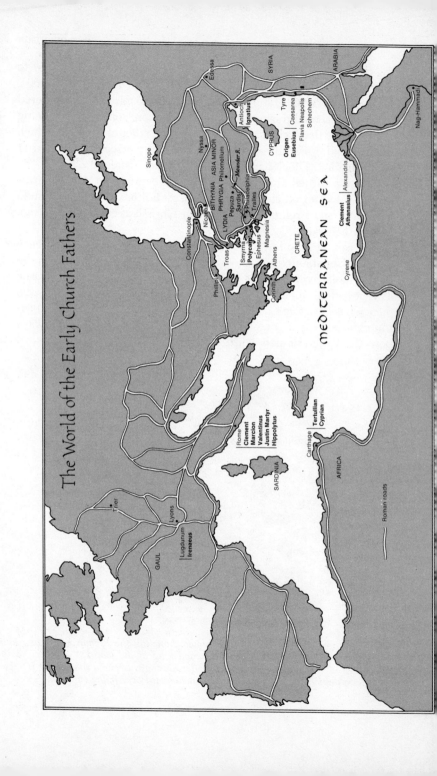

The World of the Early Church Fathers

Chapter One

Should Bygones Be Bygones?

HARRY EMERSON FOSDICK used to tell the story of a professor of history seated at a banquet next to a pretty but shallow-minded lady. After other unsuccessful attempts at conversation, the professor finally said: "Are you interested in history?" The sweet young thing replied: "Well, professor, I believe in letting bygones be bygones."

This anecdote describes the reaction of many to the study of history, including church history. The very term "history" makes them think of long, dry tables of dates; of lists of kings, emperors, and popes; and of examinations designed to test memory rather than understanding.

When church history is suggested as a topic for study, this general aversion to historical subjects is compounded by the indifference of many Protestants to the history of the church. Especially is this so of their attitude toward the history of the church between the time of the apostles and the time of the Reformation. After all, those centuries are claimed by Roman Catholicism, and during those centuries the church developed into the form against which the Protestant Reformers directed their attack. Many Protestants, therefore, are perfectly willing to consign the major portion of church history to the limbo of forgotten ages.

Where was the church before Luther?
Who cares?
Do Protestants regard themselves as members of a community that has maintained a continuous history since the days of Jesus and the apostles?
Why should they?

Have the centuries between the apostles and the Reformation anything positive to say to the church of the twentieth century? Well, do they?

The men who are called "the fathers of the early church" in this book all lived before Augustine—who died in A.D. 430. A major thesis of this work is that the lives and the thought of the early church fathers are a resource for present-day Christians in the problems and decisions of contemporary Christian life. The fathers of the early church are a neglected treasure not only for individuals but also for the modern church. Their lives and thoughts *are* relevant, not because we can automatically make their answers our answers, but because we inevitably make their questions our questions. Of course, one may be a Christian without making a study of the fathers; but such a study can make him a more sensitive, a more understanding, and a more responsible Christian. In the present state of the church, a Christian needs all the aid and counsel he can find, including that which comes from the Greek and Latin fathers.

The names of the men with whom we shall deal may be strange-sounding and unfamiliar. In this book we shall "visit," for example, with

> Clement (klĕm'ent)
> Ignatius (ĭg-nā'shĭ-us)
> Polycarp (pŏl'ĭ-kärp)
> Hermas (hŭr'mus)
> Marcion (mar'shĭ-un)
> Justin (jus'tĭn)
> Valentinus (văl'en-tī'nus)
> Irenaeus (ī-rēy-nē'us)
> Tertullian (ter-tul'yăn)
> Origen (ŏr'-ĭ-jen)
> Hippolytus (hĭ-pŏl'ĭ-tus)
> Cyprian (sĭp'rĭ-an)
> Eusebius (yoo-sē'bĭ-us)
> and Athanasius (ath'a-nā'shĭ-us).

The issues with which these men struggled, on the other hand, have all-too-familiar counterparts at the very heart of the present-day scene.

> *After the apostles, what is to be the character of the church?*
> *For what are you willing to die?*
> *Should Christians tolerate any kind of class structure?*
> *Are you a heretic?*
> *Where do ecumenical discussions locate authority?*
> *What is the role of intellectuals in the church?*
> *In Christian sexual ethics, how do you mix freedom and discipline?*
> *Is there meaning in liturgy and ritual?*

Such issues themselves are sufficient to demonstrate the relevance of the early church fathers. Their significance becomes even more apparent, however, with reference to the current situation of the Christian church. During most of its history, Christianity has occupied a position of dominance in its culture. It has shaped the education, the literature, the art, the thought, the ethics, and the very language of the nations in which it has lived. However, that period of Christian domination over culture is over, even though some remnants of it still delude people into believing that "we live in a Christian country." The centuries of Christian domination are therefore of less direct value to us than is the period of the early church, when Christianity also lived as a minority in a culture that was alien to many of the deepest affirmations of the gospel.

If modern Christians can be made to see the value of the early church for their own lives as individuals and as members of the church, the task of reconstructing the Christian witness and of renewing the Christian church in the modern age will be significantly enhanced.

A fifth-century bishop's chair (Maximianus, bishop of Ravenna, who died in 556). One of the earliest extant monuments that tells the story of Jesus continuously. (See enlarged detail on page 21.)

10

After the Apostles—What?

WHAT IS THE MEANING of the statement, in Ephesians 2:20, that the church is "built upon the foundation of the apostles and prophets"? Every effort to rethink the place of the church in the world comes up against this very question. It was a central issue in the Protestant Reformation. It is one of the thorniest problems in the ecumenical movement. In addition, it underlies many of the discussions of the relation between the local congregation, the church at large, and the ministry which have been agitating many groups.

The question is raised by the New Testament itself, for neither Jesus nor his disciples nor the apostle Paul set down detailed prescriptions for the continuation of the church.

The question of continuity is deeply intertwined with the widespread feeling among the early followers of Jesus that the Christ would soon return. Illustrative of the numerous passages of scripture that gave rise to this feeling is Matthew 10:23: "When they persecute you in one town, flee to the next; for truly, I say to you, you will not have gone through all the towns of Israel, before the Son of man comes." Also illustrative is 1 Thessalonians 4:15: "For this we declare to you by the word of the Lord, that we who are alive, who are left until the coming of the Lord, shall not precede those who have fallen asleep."

If Paul expected to be alive at the coming of Christ, it would not have seemed necessary to assure the continuation of the church after the apostolic era, for the apostolic era was also the last age. If this expectation was a mistaken one, did this mean that after the death of the last apostle the church was on its own, without directives from Christ and the apostles about the future pattern of its life?

The Earliest Father

To observe an early century struggle with such questions we can "visit" with Clement of Rome. The so-called *First Epistle of Clement* is perhaps the oldest Christian writing after the New Testament. In fact, many scholars would maintain that it is older than some of the books in the New Testament, although they would not all agree about which of these books date from the second century. The title "first epistle" is actually a misnomer; for the document sometimes called the *Second Epistle of Clement* was a sermon rather than a letter, and was not written by Clement. Thus one can speak simply of the Epistle of Clement, or more accurately, of the Epistle of Clement of Rome (to distinguish him from Clement of Alexandria, who lived a century later).

Who was Clement?

The apostle Paul, addressing the Philippians, speaks of "Clement and the rest of my fellow workers" (Philippians 4:3). The church historian Eusebius and other early Christian writers thought that this was the same Clement as the author of the epistle, but this identification seems unlikely. The same account by Eusebius also states that Clement was the third successor of Peter as bishop of Rome, following Linus and Anencletus. This is based on the list of Roman bishops presented by Irenaeus at the middle of the second century. Yet another tradition of the early church reports that Clement received the office of bishop from Peter himself, but turned it over to Linus and became bishop again only after Anencletus had died. From these various accounts it seems reasonable to conclude that Clement was indeed a bishop of Rome (though not necessarily *the* bishop) during the last decade of the first century. Other information is less reliable, and later stories about the life and death of Clement must be classified as pious fabrications.

The Epistle of Clement was written in the midst of repeated calamities and adverse experiences, at a time when Christians were being persecuted under the Emperor Domitian about A.D. 96. It was occasioned by a woeful and "godless" split that had arisen in the church at Corinth when certain members persuaded a majority of the congregation to "eject" their clergy from the sacred ministry. Clement wrote the epistle to reprimand this majority and to urge a restoration of proper order and a respect for authority. The chief themes of the epistle, therefore, are the need for harmony within the church and the need for obedience to the bishops ordained by the apostles and their successors. Clement expresses his feeling that the schism has "perverted many, many it has thrown into discouragement, many it has bewildered." [1] It has even come to the attention of people of other religious convictions, Jews and pagans, and given them occasion for blasphemies and slanders against Christians.

The Argument of the Epistle

Clement opens the epistle by recalling the reputation of the Corinthian church for harmony and humility, and by contrasting that with its present state of schism. He describes the ruinous effects of jealousy and envy, which caused the death of Abel as well as of Peter and Paul, and which have laid mighty cities low and uprooted powerful nations. Consideration of these effects should produce repentance, which God has sworn to regard. A résumé of the history of the Old Testament patriarchs proves this: Enoch, Noah, Abraham, Lot, and Rahab were obedient to their duty and were saved, while Lot's wife was turned to a pillar of salt because of her disobedience. Christians should therefore not follow the ringleaders of sedition; instead, they should humbly associate with those who cultivate peace, following above all the example set by Christ himself, and also the examples of the saints of the Old Testament like Elijah, Elisha, Ezekiel, Abraham, Job, Moses, and David.

These examples are confirmed by the testimony of the universe itself, whose regularity and harmony are evidence of its obedience to the decrees of the Creator. Similarly, Christians should not desert the place his will has assigned to them, but should practice humility and should instill it in their children. Not only the regularity of nature and history, but the imminent end of history should prompt believers to repentance and humility, for through the miracle of the seed and the strange phenomenon of the phoenix,* nature gives signs of that end and of the coming resurrection of the dead.

---

* According to ancient Egyptian legend, the phoenix is a legendary bird that lived five or six centuries in the Arabian desert. It was then consumed in fire through its own act, and rose again with youthful energy from its remaining ashes. Thus the phoenix often stands as the symbol of immortality or of the resurrection.

The faithfulness of God and the universality of his sovereignty summon Christians to holiness of soul, purity of morals, mildness, humility, and gentleness of spirit. Once again the history of the Old Testament echoes this divine summons to obedience. Through Christ the High Priest, God has brought salvation and enlightenment, and has enlisted believers in his army.

In that army there is a variety of rank, just as in the human body all the parts belong together in an organic unity. In the church, therefore, each must respect both the special endowments and the official position of the other. The worship of the church should be offered at stated times and by authorized persons, as Moses showed in the Old Testament through the miracle of the rod of Aaron. (See Exodus 4:1–17.) Thus the apostles appointed their successors and these, in turn, were succeeded by others, whom it is not right to depose. The Corinthians should, therefore, forsake their schism and return to the holy practice of brotherly love; for it was love that moved Christ to die for men, and love will endure forever. Those who have been guilty of loveless conduct should repent and confess their sin. Instead of self-aggrandizement, they should ponder the experiences and examples of Moses, of Judith and Esther, and even of pagan rulers, who have sacrificed their own well-being for the sake of others. They should accept reproof and submit to the clergy at Corinth. Scripture warns the disobedient, but promises salvation to those who obey the will of God. May God grant peace, harmony, and an obedient will to all men, and may the Corinthians regain tranquillity in their own congregation.

The Outcome

There is no direct information available about the outcome of Clement's correspondence with the Corinthians. About A.D. 170, however, Dionysius, bishop of Corinth, informed Soter, bishop of Rome, that the Epistle of Clement was being read in his church. This suggests that the epistle was well received and that it accomplished its end. The use of the epistle as sacred reading was not confined to Corinth. Eusebius informed his readers that it "has been publicly used in a great many churches both in former times and in our own." [2] As we have seen, in addition to the epistle, a second epistle and a large body of other apocryphal literature were attributed to Clement in later times; but no modern scholar accepts this theory.

14

By the time Clement wrote his so-called first epistle, the church at Corinth—as well as the church at Rome—had clearly acquired forms and structures in its organizational life that were more stable than the ones seen in the New Testament. Any extensive reflection, however, moves one into an assessment of the necessity and the correctness of these forms and patterns. Did the church "fall" when it developed an organization? In what sense could the bishop rightly claim to stand in a continuous line with the apostles? Even if he could, was this any guarantee that the church was "apostolic"? After the apostles, and in the present time, what is to be authoritative and definitive in guiding the order and structure of the church? This was, and is, a question of such importance that it warrants extensive consideration.

PONT. COMM. DI ARCH. SACRA

A third-century gravestone in the catacomb of Callistus. Clement spoke of the anchor as the symbol of salvation. The fish is a symbol for Jesus Christ.

15

An early church bishop bestowing the veil on a virgin.
The act is an example of the far-ranging authority of the bishop.
"Do nothing without the bishop" was one of Ignatius' maxims.

The Humanity of Jesus

In Ignatius' dealing with the faith and life of the Christian community, the key issue seems to have been the historical humanity of Jesus. If the teachings of Jesus rather than his death and resurrection form the basis of certain kinds of Christian faith, why is it so important to hold out for the fact that he was truly human, or for that matter that he ever actually lived? If his teachings are true, do they not continue to be true even if there is no "biography" of Jesus?

Ignatius cautioned the churches to be alert to the existence and to the importance of the issue. He called for them to examine both the historical humanity and the teachings of Jesus, and he pleaded with them to find ways for each of these two positions to meet the challenge addressed by the other position.

Enlarged detail of a panel from a fifth-century bishop's chair (see chair on page 10). The panel depicts Christ healing the blind and the lame.

The ultimate protest. With the aid of fellow Buddhist monks, Thich Quang Duc commits suicide by fire in the streets of Saigon. Tension between loyalty to God and loyalty to state was a major factor in producing martyrdom in early centuries. Men like Polycarp and Ignatius, as well as Peter and Paul, struggled with this problem. In his Letter to the Philippians, Paul wrote: "With full courage now as always Christ will be honored in my body, whether by life or by death. For to me to live is Christ, and to die is gain. If it is to be life in the flesh, that means fruitful labor for me. Yet which I shall choose I cannot tell. I am hard pressed between the two" (1:20–23). Christians cannot escape the inevitable question of what they are willing to die for.

stand squarely on the decrees of the Lord and the apostles, being submissive to the bishop and to one another in Christ for the sake of unity.

The third of the epistles written by Ignatius from Smyrna is directed to the congregation at Tralles, also in the valley of the Maeander. The doctrine against which it specially warns, however, is not Judaism, but the heresy that came to be called Docetism, the denial of the full and true humanity of Jesus Christ. After commending the congregation for their harmony and their loyalty to the bishop, therefore, Ignatius warns them to abstain from "plants of alien growth"; that is to say, from heresy. He has in mind the heresy of those who say that "his [Christ's] suffering was but a make-believe" and who deny that he was really born, that he really ate and drank, that he was really persecuted by Pontius Pilate, that he was really crucified, and that he really rose from the dead. Such plants bear poisonous and deadly fruit, as anyone must who is apart from the oneness of the church, which is maintained by love and unity with the bishop and the presbytery. The love and intercession of the Christians sustain the writer as he faces the prospect of witnessing through martyrdom.

The prospect of martyrdom is the primary theme of the epistle to the Romans, also penned at Smyrna. It opens with a much greater spirit of praise than that of any of the other Ignatian letters. Whether this is due to a position of primacy or to the wealth and generosity of the Roman church has been a matter of controversy between Roman Catholics and Protestants, as has, for that matter, the authenticity of all the epistles. Looking forward to a personal meeting with the members in Rome, Ignatius expresses his fear that the congregation may cheat him of his martyr's crown. "God has graciously summoned the bishop of Syria to come from the rising of the sun to the setting. How glorious to be a setting sun—away from the world, on to God! May I rise in his presence!" [4]

Ignatius is not an apostle with the right to issue orders as Peter and Paul were, but he is on his way to being a disciple. Christ has suffered for men, and now Ignatius wants to imitate his suffering. Even if, in a moment of weakness, he should ask for the intervention of the Roman Christians, they must not listen. Both he himself and his orphaned Syrian church require the *prayers* of the Christians in the mighty city of Rome.

19

The Epistles from Troas

Less personal than the epistles from Smyrna, but equally passionate in its devotion to the central concerns of the faith and life of the church, is the Epistle to the Philadelphians—one of the seven churches of Asia to which the book of Revelation had also been addressed. (See Revelation 1:4 ff.) This church, too, is praised for its loyalty to its bishop and clergy, and warned to shun all schism and dissension. Ignatius finds his consolation in the gospel and in the apostles and prophets, all of whom, even and especially the prophets, bear witness to the superiority of Christ over Judaism. His exhortation to unity is caused not by any knowledge he may have of their church, but by his conviction that where there is division and passion, there is no place for God. Above the prophets, the apostles, the bishops, the church—even above the Scriptures—is Christ himself, who is also the common hope.

While at Troas, Ignatius also wrote a letter to the church at Smyrna and another to Polycarp, its bishop. Once more he takes pains to insist on the reality of the humanity of Christ, in opposition to those who call it a make-believe. If it was a make-believe, both the faith of the apostles and the martyrdom of Ignatius are all illusion. "What good does anyone do me if he praises me, but blasphemes my Lord by not admitting that he carried living flesh about him?"[5] Those who deny this also neglect the works of Christian charity and the public worship of the church. Such men are to be avoided in turn. Only in fellowship with the bishop can the church remain with Christ, and "where Jesus Christ is, there is the Catholic church."[6] (This is the earliest known instance of the word "Catholic.") The letter to the Christians at Smyrna closes with thanks for their concern about the church in Syria, and with greetings and farewells.

The letter to Polycarp is the shortest of the Ignatian epistles, but it manages to sound most of their themes. As bishop, Polycarp has responsibility for the spiritual life and unity of his people. This requires pastoral care and constant attention to preaching and teaching about the moral duties of Christians. A Christian is not his own master. A Christian's time belongs to God. In conclusion, Polycarp is asked to convey instructions and regards from Ignatius to all the churches.

For What Are You Willing to Die?

WHAT IS THE SIGNIFICANCE of any definition of martyrdom for Christian living in an affluent and tolerant society—a forbearing society that has an abundant supply of material possessions?

Do you regard the early Christian martyrs as heroes? If so, how do you regard the absence of martyrdom in the American churches of the present day? Is this evidence of flabbiness and unfaithfulness?

Or, on the other hand, are you inclined to minimize the importance of martyrdom in the life of the church? If so, do you believe that in a time of crisis the Christian churches of America would or should produce martyrs?

There has, after all, been more persecution of Christians in our century than in any since the ancient church! Some Christians have been martyred, some have escaped, and some have compromised with the enemy.

For what are you willing to die?

Instructed by the Apostles

From the epistles of Ignatius we already know about one of the most remarkable men of the early church—Polycarp of Smyrna. Because his long life spans the period of transition from the apostles to the "Old-Catholic Church" seen in the writings of Irenaeus at the end of the second century, Polycarp deserves to be studied as more than merely a correspondent of Ignatius.

Writing perhaps between A.D. 180 and 190, Irenaeus spoke of Polycarp as follows: "Polycarp was not only instructed by apostles, and conversed with many who had seen Christ, but was also, by apostles in Asia, appointed bishop of the church in Smyrna, whom

23

I also saw in my earliest youth, for he tarried [on earth] a very long time, and, when a very old man, gloriously and most nobly suffering martyrdom, departed this life, having always taught the things which he had learned from the apostles, and which the church has handed down, and which alone are true." [1] If we are to believe this account, Polycarp must have been born no later than the third quarter of the first century. The apostle John, with whom Polycarp was associated, is said by tradition to have been the only apostle who died a natural death, and that presumably before the end of the first century. As for his death, the date of the martyrdom of Polycarp has long been a subject of controversy, and it would be foolhardy to say that the last word on the question has been spoken. However, it seems to have taken place in either A.D. 156 or 167.

Epistle to the Philippians

Although most of our scanty information about Polycarp comes from the epistles of Ignatius, from Irenaeus and Eusebius, and from *The Martyrdom of Polycarp* (to be discussed later), we do have one writing that bears his name. According to some scholars, it is actually a blending of two writings by Polycarp. In the manuscripts it bears the title: "The epistle of St. Polycarp, bishop of Smyrna and holy martyr, to the Philippians." The epistle is a rehearsal of familiar and traditional materials, justifying the judgment of one historian that he was most obviously a man that lived in the past.

Opening his epistle to the Philippians with a recollection of the epistle addressed to them by the apostle Paul, Polycarp commends them for their faithfulness and urges them to obey the commandments of Jesus. Believers in each walk of life have their special temptations and particular duties. Young people of both sexes are exhorted to keep themselves pure. Special admonition has to do with the clergy, who set an example for the whole congregation and who have a responsibility for pastoral care.

Polycarp attacks heretics who deny the reality of the humanity of Jesus or who say that there is neither a resurrection nor a judgment. He urges the Philippians to exercise patience and to persevere in doing good. Referring to the case of a certain Valens, who had been a presbyter in Philippi but had fallen into sin, Polycarp prays that Valens may be truly penitent and the congregation truly forgiving. Finally, he prays for the congregation and asks prayer for others.

The Martyrdom of Polycarp

Much more sympathetic and appealing a document is *The Martyrdom of Polycarp*, a short novel in the form of an encyclical letter addressed "from the church which sojourns at Smyrna" to the church at Philomelium and "to all the sojournings of the holy and Catholic church in every place." Portions of it—including the chapter giving the date of Polycarp's martyrdom as well as of the composition of the epistle—seem to have been altered and changed from the original. Therefore some critics have been inclined to suspect that *The Martyrdom* itself was not written in the second century, as it purports to be, but later.

This skepticism has not proved persuasive to most scholars, however, and we are probably justified in regarding *The Martyrdom* not only as the earliest postbiblical account of the death of a martyr, but as a reliable, if somewhat romanticized, narrative—especially as compared with the extravagant reports of miracles and of heroism in the later Acts of the Martyrs. Eusebius cites *The Martyrdom* at great length in his *Ecclesiastical History*.

The opening chapters of *The Martyrdom* announce its theme: the nobleness of mind, the patience, and the love for their Lord displayed by all the martyrs and above all by Polycarp. Such a hero of the faith was Germanicus, whose willingness to be devoured by a wild beast caused the bloodthirsty mob to cry for more: "Away with the atheists! Let Polycarp be sought out!" [2] Persuaded by others to take flight, Polycarp was betrayed to his pursuers and arrested. The purpose of all of this was "that he might fulfill his special lot, being made a partaker of Christ, and that they who betrayed him might undergo the punishment of Judas himself." [3]

Polycarp's captors tried to convince him that offering pagan sacrifices and acknowledging the lordship of Caesar was not to be magnified out of proportion to its true importance, and that he should take this easy way out. However, he refused. When he was brought into the stadium for trial and execution, the proconsul—governor, or military commander—gave him one last chance to stop resisting and speak against Christ. Polycarp's answer, which has since become classic, was: "For six and eighty years I have been serving him, and he has done no wrong to me. How, then, dare I blaspheme my King who has saved me?" [4]

25

Further prodding and threatening proved useless, and the proconsul announced to the mob in the stadium that Polycarp had confessed that he was a Christian. So Polycarp was condemned to death by fire. On the pyre Polycarp remained constant, thanking God "because you have seen fit to bestow on me this day and this hour, that I may share, among the number of the martyrs, the cup of your Anointed and rise to eternal life both in soul and in body, in virtue of the immortality of the Holy Spirit. May I be accepted among them in your sight today as a rich and pleasing sacrifice!" [5] When he had spoken this Amen, the fire was ignited. The flames, however, did not harm him, and he had to be stabbed to death by an executioner. The Romans refused to surrender Polycarp's body to his fellow-believers, burning it until only his bones remained; these were gathered up and preserved by the congregation at Smyrna for the annual observance of the day of his martyrdom. The Smyrnaeans asked their readers to circulate the epistle among all the other churches.

The children in the fiery furnace, one of the earliest and most prevalent themes in catacomb art. The portrayal symbolizes salvation.

Chapter Five

THE SHEPHERD OF HERMAS

Revelations Stressing Repentance

ALL THE WRITINGS of the fathers discussed so far, even *The Martyrdom of Polycarp,* are epistles. They follow the example of most of the books of the New Testament and of classical letter-writing, which has been called "next to satire, Rome's most distinctive legacy to the world's literature." [1] When we turn from them to *The Shepherd of Hermas,* we are in quite another literary tradition. Not the letters of Paul and John, but the Revelation of John is the typical model here.

The Shepherd of Hermas is an apocalypse. "Apocalypse" means revelation, and that is just what *The Shepherd* is—a series of revelations granted to Hermas and in turn given by him to the church. The first portion of the book consists of five visions; the second of twelve mandates, or commandments; the third of ten parables, or similitudes.

About the external facts of the author's biography we are even less informed than about those of the other early church fathers. Documentary analysis of the book has suggested to some recent scholars that more than one author is responsible for *The Shepherd.* Even the more conservative among scholars are inclined to believe that the revelations, though the work of only one man, were composed over a period of many years. It is generally agreed that the reference to Rome as the author's residence is probably trustworthy.

Both in message and in style, *The Shepherd* makes it clear that the author regarded himself as the possessor of special prophetic gifts. Even the very absence of specific references to "prophets" alongside "apostles" and "teachers" in the ministry of the church substantiates this impression. Hermas passed over the prophets because he considered himself one of them. This role of latter-day prophet and seer is essential to any understanding of the tone and figurative language of *The Shepherd*. Like the Apocalypse or Revelation of the New Testament, it has been subjected to repeated and involved interpretation of each individual metaphor. The result has been a loss of attention to the characteristic mixing and heaping up of metaphors found in much apocalyptic literature.

Modern readers may not find this literature congenial. For example, the most celebrated of current theologies of the New Testament contains exactly two references to the book of Revelation among its hundreds of citations of the New Testament. Pleasing or not, apocalypse as a literary form and as a religious experience was an essential element of early Christianity. In fact, it was perhaps more essential than the few remaining apocalypses would indicate, since the disfavor into which apocalypticism fell may have caused some of them to be lost.

Although a summary of visions, mandates, and parables of *The Shepherd of Hermas* cannot be expected to reproduce the distinctive flavor of Hermas, it may serve as a guide to study.

The Visions

In the first vision Hermas beholds an aged matron dressed in a bright robe and seated on a huge chair of white wool. When Hermas confesses to her that he feels guilty for having desired a woman, the matron assures him that God is not angry with him on this account; and she reads to him from the book she holds in her hand, summoning him to repent.

The second vision reveals to Hermas that the aged matron is not a prophetic oracle, or mysterious divine revelation. Rather, the aged matron symbolizes the church. Hermas asks for her permission to copy the book she holds. The book declares: "Filled up are the days of repentance to all the saints; but to the heathen, repentance will be possible even to the last day." [2]

Further disclosures about the church come with the third vision, in which Hermas sees a stone tower in the process of construction. Some stones are fitted together so smoothly that they look like one stone. Others are rejected. Still others are cut down to size. This symbolizes the unity of the church, but also its purity, which requires that sinners repent of their evil.

The central apparition in the fourth vision is a huge monster, as big as a whale, representing the persecution that will soon come upon the church. The church appears in the vision too, however, adorned as a bride. This shows that those who are faithful and pure will not be harmed by the persecution.

With the fifth and final vision we meet the shepherd for whom the book is named. Hermas is entrusted to his guidance—to receive the commandments that form the second part of the apocalypse.

The Mandates

The first of the mandates or commandments is to "believe that there is one God who created and finished all things, and made all things out of nothing. He alone is able to contain the whole, but himself cannot be contained."[3] On this basis the second mandate commands innocence and simplicity of heart, especially in the practice of charity. In the third mandate the shepherd denounces falsehood, and when Hermas confesses that he has made a habit of falsehood, reproaches him and summons him to mend his ways. Similarly, the fourth mandate condemns sexual immorality by a married woman. Hermas asks whether such a sin of adultery committed by a baptized person can ever be forgiven. In the mandate it is explained that some teachers maintain that there can be no forgiveness of sins after baptism. The answer of the commandment is that one remission after baptism may be granted. The sin dealt with in the fifth mandate is anger and impatience, which is censured because it will crowd the Holy Spirit out of the heart if it is left unchecked.

Expounding at greater length what was meant by some of the earlier mandates, the sixth mandate describes the power of the two angels, one of righteousness and the other of iniquity, that attend every man. Their presence can be discerned by the works they produce. The issue in the seventh mandate is fear, which properly should be of God alone and not of the devil, who is actually powerless. The requirements and prohibitions of the eighth mandate are even more general: the individual is to practice self-restraint when tempted by various vices, but need not restrain himself in the performance of good deeds.

Echoing the denunciation in James 1:7–8, the ninth mandate declares that "every double-minded man, even if he repents, will be

Representation of different ways that lead to everlasting life or eternal damnation, prepared in Pennsylvania in the early nineteenth century. The elaborate imagery and the stress on repentance are reminiscent of biblical and early Christian apocalyptic literature such as The Revelation to John *and* The Shepherd of Hermas.

saved only with difficulty."[4] Doubt has no place in the Christian life of prayer and trust. The sister of doubt and anger is grief; and the tenth mandate warns that it, too, can crush the Holy Spirit in the believer.

With the eleventh mandate Hermas apparently seeks to set himself apart from the excesses of apocalyptic revelation, for it is a warning against false prophets. The twelfth and final mandate is a summary admonition to refrain from evil desires so that we may live to God.

The Parables

The third major section of *The Shepherd* is longer than the first two combined. It consists of ten similitudes, or to use their original Greek title, parables. The message of the first parable, or similitude, is a familiar motif of early Christian thought: believers are strangers in this world and should live as the citizens of another world. The vision of a fruitful vine being supported by an elm that has no fruit of its own but that enables the vine to produce becomes, in the second parable, a picture of the relation between rich and poor: the intercessions of the poor support the rich, even though the latter appear more productive. Another parable from the vegetable world appears in the third similitude. During the winter it is impossible to tell healthy trees from withered ones. So the righteous and unrighteous are indistinguishable in the present age. On the other hand, declares the fourth similitude, the situation will be quite the reverse in the age to come where, as in the summer, the distinction will become obvious.

In the fifth parable, Hermas turns to the Christian practice of fasting, using a similitude about a vineyard to make the point that "fasting is very good, provided the commandments of the Lord be observed. . . . First of all, be on your guard against every evil word, and every evil desire, and purify your heart from all the vanities of this world. If you guard against these things, your fastings will be perfect."[5]

Not one, but two shepherds appear in the sixth similitude, symbolizing self-indulgence and punishment. They show that an individual is punished many times over for each act of self-indulgence, but that he can be saved if he repents. At the beginning of the seventh similitude Hermas complains that he is being unjustly tormented by the shepherd of punishment. He receives the explanation that it is not for his own sins but for those of his household that this punishment is being visited upon him. Even those who have repented must still go through suffering. That same idea of repentance and punishment seems to be the basic point of the eighth similitude. Twigs have been pruned from a large and flourishing willow tree; nevertheless, they go on thriving. In the same way some of those who have been separated from the law of God can find life again if by repentance they return to the source of their life.

The ninth similitude recurs to the vision of the stone tower; but instead of merely distinguishing between the stones that are accepted and those that are rejected, as the third vision did, this parable gives a detailed description of the many nations and generations from whom the stones are to come and for whom the time of repentance is being extended. The vision of the tower is carried over into the tenth similitude, which forms the conclusion of the entire work and leaves the reader with the admonition: "On your account the work of building was suspended. Unless, then, you make haste to do rightly, the tower will be completed, and you will be excluded." [6]

Status and Message

In his book *Against the Heresies*, to which we shall be referring in chapter nine, Irenaeus calls *The Shepherd of Hermas* "scripture." Eusebius reports that there were some who disputed its right to this designation, while it was adjudged as essential by others. Ironically, postbiblical prophecy, against whose distortions the eleventh mandate was directed, became so unpopular and disliked that the authority of *The Shepherd*—and in some places even that of the Revelation of John—was destroyed. Athanasius (see chapter sixteen), to whose "Easter Letter of 373" we owe much of our information about the bringing together of the New Testament canon (authoritative literature composed after the birth of Christ and accepted by the church as Holy Scripture), tells us that at the time when he wrote that letter *The Shepherd* was not included in the canon. Yet he himself, in an earlier writing, calls it a most edifying book.

The apocalyptic extravagance, or the overabundance of revelatory imagery, of *The Shepherd of Hermas* is a good reminder of the distance between the early church and ourselves. As with the Revelation of John, *The Shepherd* is literature from the life of a church in a time of so much persecution and other danger that it was necessary to write its messages in code meaningful only to those within the small band of the initiated. To Christians living without persecution, in the midst of a tolerant and flabby culture, this raises serious questions about the comparison between commitment and costly witness of the underground Christian church of ancient times and the power and commitment of a tolerated and tolerant church in the world of today. To Christians living increasingly in persecution and in costly intolerance (such as in the current struggle for human dignity and civil rights), it immediately becomes a rallying point and a source of identification with the Christians of early years.

To all Christians and to all human beings, the emphasis of *The Shepherd of Hermas* on the chronic need for repentance is a good reminder that the distance between the early church and ourselves is considerably less than infinite.

An early Christian drawing on a stone in the cemetery of Saint Callistus in Rome.

Chapter Six
MARCION

What Is Heresy?

CLEMENT, IGNATIUS, POLYCARP, AND HERMAS are all recognized as "fathers" by later Christian orthodoxy—by later official church formulations of the truth. The first three were designated saints, not by the process of canonization now in use but by the consensus of the early church. Hermas was not designated a saint, though his book was—as we have seen—thought worthy of inclusion in the Bible by some early Christians.

Yet a view of the early church based only on the writings of those who have a reputation for orthodoxy would be seriously out of focus. It is, in fact, a distortion even to credit the "orthodox fathers" and the New Testament writers with a greater measure of unity than they actually possessed. For "unless he is obsessed by a preconceived theory, [any fair-minded student] will be compelled to reckon with this genuine and far-reaching diversity in the religion of the New Testament." [1]

We tend to find the word "heretic" hard to accept. It is symptomatic of the way orthodox Christianity has developed that the term "heresy-hunter," like the term "witch-hunter," is generally used to refer to an artificial issue, invented for the sake of advancing the ambition of a church leader.

Nevertheless, there is such a thing as heresy, and there has been heresy within the Christian movement almost from the beginning. When we consider the whole spectrum of early Christianity, we have to reckon with great diversity. This has always been the case and always will be. The thorny question is: When is the diversity within the spectrum of acceptability and productive of vitality and growth, and when is the diversity abnormal, unhealthy, and in need of denunciation and surgical removal?

Even in the New Testament there is evidence that heresies and heretics were already threatening the church. Although it would be possible to reconstruct certain aspects of their teaching from a book like the Gospel of John, a more direct approach to the heresies of the first century can be obtained through some of the New Testament epistles, notably the Epistle to the Colossians and the Epistles of John.

> For many deceivers have gone out into the world, men who will not acknowledge the coming of Jesus Christ in the flesh; such a one is the deceiver and the antichrist. Look to yourselves, that you may not lose what you have worked for, but may win a full reward. Any one who goes ahead and does not abide in the doctrine of Christ does not have God; he who abides in the doctrine of Christ has both the Father and the Son. If any one comes to you and does not bring this doctrine, do not receive him into the house or give him any greeting; for he who greets him shares his wicked work.
>
> *2 John 7–11*

> Therefore let no one pass judgment on you in questions of food and drink or with regard to a festival or a new moon or a sabbath. These are only a shadow of what is to come; but the substance belongs to Christ. Let no one disqualify you, insisting on self-abasement and worship of angels, taking his stand on visions, puffed up without reason by his sensuous mind, and not holding fast to the Head, from whom the whole body, nourished and knit together through its joints and ligaments, grows with a growth that is from God.
>
> *Colossians 2:16–19*

While it may be interesting to consider what manner of teaching is being denounced here, it is more important to note the fact that as soon as the Christian movement began to take shape, there arose distortions of its teaching serious enough to call forth such denunciations. Entirely apart from one or another specific controversy, a responsible consideration of the challenges to Christian teaching will probably lead most observers to the conclusion that the church had both a right and an obligation to repudiate any teacher who distorted the Christian message in a fundamental way. It will undoubtedly also lead most sober observers to question the implications of this early church history for the present-day life of the church. If the church had this right and obligation then, what about the contemporary scene?

Gnosticism

The very church fathers who acquired a reputation for orthodoxy did so at least in part by their defense of normative Christian belief against not only its detractors from without (Jews and pagans) but also against its distorters from within (schismatics and heretics). The word "heresy" in the sense of false teaching seems to have been used for the first time by Ignatius. In most instances when the fathers of the second century used the word, they were referring to one or another species of Gnosticism, a virile and subtle competitor of early Christianity.

Gnosticism was not confined to Christianity. It existed prior to the coming of Christ, and it was highly syncretistic. That is, it believed in taking advantage of contributions from many sources, and it assumed many forms. The height of its influence was from about A.D. 135 to 160. In the second century, it was so widely embraced that for a time many of those who regarded themselves as Christians apparently adhered to one or another of its many forms.

Gnostics believed in a *gnosis*, which was not a philosophy derived from man's striving but a revealed knowledge—a revealed knowledge transmitted to those who have been initiated. Followers of the movement could point to such statements as that which Jesus is represented as saying in John 16:12: "I have yet many things to say to you, but you cannot bear them now." This suggests that Jesus reserved certain truths for a more opportune time than even his last days on earth. When the same Gospel declares that "Jesus did many other signs in the presence of the disciples, which are not written in this book" (John 20:30), it is understandable that the early Christians, who were eager for every scrap of information about the life and teachings of their Lord, should have wondered where, if anywhere, these "many other signs" were remembered, described, and recorded.

In a sense, therefore, Gnosticism has the fascination that some persons find in a secret which is disclosed only to a privileged few. It is a club for the ultrasophisticated who feel sorry for those who simply are not "with it." Interpreted in this manner, the question of whether or not Gnosticism is operative in the present-day church is a live and significant query.

Until quite recently, students of early Christianity have been dependent for their knowledge of the Gnostics on the arguments of the church fathers against Gnosticism, with the addition of a few authentic Gnostic writings. In 1945, however, an entire library of Gnostic treatises was discovered at Nag-Hammadi in Egypt. Those portions of the library that have been published thus far have already helped to make Gnosticism one of the most exciting areas in current historical research. There are at least some scholars who say that whole chapters in our conventional histories of the early church may have to be rewritten as a consequence. Even so brief

Gnostic seal typical of amulets used to protect wearer from forces of evil.

an introduction to the church fathers as the present one cannot ignore Gnosticism.

Although the Gnostics with whom the church fathers dealt and about whom we are best informed were all influenced by Christian thought, the sources of Gnosticism were quite diverse. "It seems to have arisen out of a mixture of Hellenistic, Jewish, Oriental, and Christian factors, combined in an atmosphere of intense otherworldliness and imaginative myth-making." [2] In part, the variations among Gnostic systems can be explained by the various proportions in this mixture, but the major Gnostic teachers were also creative thinkers.

Another feature of Gnosticism was that it regarded pure spirit as good, but thought of that spirit as being imprisoned in corrupt matter. Material elements and flesh were regarded as evil. Salvation was the freeing of the spirit from the flesh. In regard to Jesus, this led to an extreme de-emphasis upon his humanity, if not to an outright denial. The Redeemer must have nothing of the taint of the flesh—which is evil.

This is really a kind of Docetism, a dualism which separates the Christ into spirit and body. Docetism maintains that Jesus appeared in a spiritual body, and that he had no actual body; therefore, he only seemed to suffer and die on the cross.

Marcion

Marcion was born sometime early in the second century, in the ancient city of Sinope on the Black Sea. Some later accounts claim that his father was a bishop and that Marcion was excommunicated by him because of fornication. There is some suspicion, however, that this is merely part of the usual case against the heretic as both a subverter of the truth and a perverter of the young. More plausible is the report that Marcion was a shipowner and became wealthy. Sometime before A.D. 140 he came to Rome, to whose church he made an extremely generous contribution. After his arrival in Rome he developed and began to set forth doctrines that diverged from those held by most Roman Christians, and in July 144 he was excommunicated. Nevertheless, he continued to propagate his heretical opinions, which had already gained support during the second century in places as widely scattered as Asia Minor, Lydia, Bithynia, Corinth, Crete, Antioch, Alexandria, Rome, Lyons, and Carthage. Thus during the second half of the second century, Marcion's sect, "and it alone, was really a rival church" to the orthodox.[3] The seriousness of its threat is evident from the sheer number of orthodox refutations it called forth. Marcion seems to have died about A.D. 160, but his movement survived him and remnants continued into the Middle Ages.

Marcion insisted that the Christian church had obscured the gospel by seeking to combine Christianity with Judaism. He maintained that the God of the Old Testament and of the Jews is an evil God. Referring to the words of Jesus that a good tree cannot bring forth evil fruit, he argued that a world which contains the suffering which is everywhere apparent must be the work of an evil being rather than of a good God. Marcion contended, further, that in contrast with the God of the Jews there is a second God, hidden until revealed in Jesus the Christ.

According to Adolf Harnack, whose book on Marcion continues to be the basic work in the field despite the need for some necessary criticisms, the fundamental issue for Marcion was the radical distinction between the Christian gospel and all other or previous religions. "Wonder of wonders," wrote Marcion, "that one cannot say anything at all about the gospel, nor think about it, nor compare it with anything!"[4]

The vicious massacre of the Jews in A.D. 135 may have been what prompted Marcion to ponder especially the novelty of the gospel in relation to Judaism. He drew a sharp contrast between the message of love in the New Testament and the emphasis of the Old Testament on law and justice. In this contrast he found evidence of a vastly deeper cleavage that reached into the Divine itself. The God of the Old Testament was a God of justice and of wrath, but the Father of our Lord Jesus Christ was a God of love and mercy. There must, then, be two Gods—the lesser God of Judaism and the supreme God revealed in the gospel. But the God of the Old Testament is also presented as the Creator of heaven and earth. Did this mean that the universe was produced by a deity other than, and inferior to, the supreme God? Marcion was not afraid to follow his ideas consistently to this drastic conclusion.

Yet the New Testament takes great pains to point out its continuities with the Old. Jesus said he had come not to abolish the Law and the Prophets but to fulfill them (see Matthew 5:17). The apostle Paul had specifically identified the God who said "Let light shine out of darkness" at the beginning of creation with the God who had "shone in our hearts" (2 Corinthians 4:6). To come to terms with this contradiction of his gospel, Marcion concluded that the writings which were circulating as Christian scripture (which had not yet, of course, been clearly delimited as a canon) had been tampered with. It was clear from the records that the disciples of Jesus had not understood him at many crucial points. That misunderstanding was reflected in the Gospels that claimed to be accounts of his ministry and teaching. Of these only that of Luke was authentic; and it, too, had been mutilated and altered by those who did not see the disjunction or discontinuity between the Old Testament and the New. Similarly, several counterfeit epistles were claiming apostolic authority, and even those epistles of Paul which were genuine contained clever additions that distorted their sense.

Marcion, therefore, took it upon himself to produce a purified collection of Christian writings, which may have hastened the production of the orthodox canon of the New Testament. Thus Marcion put himself forward as a restorer of true Christianity. He differed from most Gnostics in his lack of interest in myths concerning the universe, but he shared with them the contrast between the flesh and the spirit that characterized their theology and their ethics.

Chapter Seven
VALENTINUS

Should Christians Tolerate Classes?

As WE HAVE SEEN in chapter three, the word "Catholic" was first used in connection with the church by Ignatius. He employed it in the untechnical sense of universal. However, the aggressive attacks upon the church by such forces as Gnosticism served to create a strongly consolidated church. The power of the bishops was greatly strengthened, a collection of authoritative New Testament scripture was recognized, and a creed was formulated. This strongly consolidated church, which developed its distinguishing characteristics during the crises of the second century, is now usually referred to as the Old-Catholic Church. A "visit" with Valentinus will provide us with an opportunity to look in on some of the controversy out of which the Old-Catholic Church grew. It will also raise certain questions about contemporary church practices, especially about whether or not Christians should tolerate a class structure.

Church fathers like Irenaeus frequently link Valentinus with Marcion and think of them as the founders of the principal schools of Christian Gnostics. Discussing the untraditional character of the doctrines of Marcion and Valentinus, Irenaeus writes: "Prior to Valentinus, those who follow Valentinus had no existence. . . . For Valentinus came to Rome in the time of Hyginus, flourished under Pius, and remained until Anicetus." [1] This would place his activities in Rome in the period beginning before A.D. 140 (when Marcion also seems to have arrived there) until just before A.D. 160. According to the later account of Epiphanius, Valentinus had originally come from a family in Egypt and from an education in Alexandria. Epiphanius reports also that after leaving Rome, Valentinus taught on the Island of Cyprus. But in evaluating the importance of this

41

claim, it must be remembered that Epiphanius himself was a Cypriote. Tertullian claimed that "Valentinus had expected to become bishop [of Rome], because he was an able man both in genius and eloquence," but that "he broke with the church of the true faith" when he was not elected.[2] Beyond these scraps of information, there is very little that we know about the life of Valentinus; and because the information comes from anti-Gnostic sources, we may not really "know" even this much.

About Valentinian teaching, on the other hand, we are probably entitled to speak at greater length, especially if we include under "Valentinian teaching" the doctrines of Ptolemy, a second-century astronomer, mathematician, and geographer. Ptolemy's "Letter to Flora," incorporated into the anti-Gnostic treatise of Epiphanius, was one of the few Gnostic writings available before the discoveries at Nag-Hammadi. Those discoveries have added to the store of source material on Valentinian Gnosticism a book to which Irenaeus refers as the *Gospel of Truth,* an ironic title in light of the fact that the book almost never agrees with the Gospels of the New Testament. It seems quite certain that we now have the text of that *Gospel of Truth,* though it is in a Coptic translation. Although it probably does not embody the unadulterated teachings of Valentinus but combines them with the speculations of his followers, it is a useful supplement to the data on Valentinian Gnosticism available from those other sources.

For our purposes here it is perhaps permissible to treat "Valentinian Gnosticism" as an entity, even though we know that there were serious changes in the course of the development of the system. We shall have occasion to mention at least a few of these changes as well.

Valentinian Teachings

The Valentinian system begins with the idea of an Aeon, or Ultimate—a divine being who dwells in invisible elevations and who is eternal and ungenerated. An "aeon" is an immeasurable or infinite period of time, and the Aeon (Ultimate) dwells in divine unity and deep solitude for infinite aeons.

This divine unity or solitude is broken by a series of emanations, or radiations, that proceed from the abyss of the divine dwelling place. These emanations, or radiations, usually called "aeons," are produced in pairs until there are finally thirty of them, corresponding to the thirty days thought to comprise the lunar month.

In an effort to spiritualize the account of creation given in the book of Genesis, the Valentinians have explained creation by emanation, and have shifted the scene from this universe to the one above. Out of these emanations there eventually emerged the Creator—the Greek name used by Valentinians is *Demiurge,* which calls to mind the *Timaeus* of Plato—who was responsible for the origin of the material world. Thus the Valentinians, like Marcion, made a sharp distinction between the Ultimate (Aeon) and the Creator (Demiurge). The Demiurge "made heaven without knowing heaven; he formed man in ignorance of man; he brought earth to light without understanding earth." [3]

Man, then, is the creature not of the supreme God (Ultimate), but of the Demiurge (Creator). In fact, in the *Gospel of Truth* it is a personification of error and deception, *Plane,* to whom the act of creation is ascribed. We are told that *Plane* set to work upon her substance in a void, in ignorance of the truth. Later Valentinian theology, as reported by Irenaeus, recounted the myth that, unknown to the Demiurge (Creator), something spiritual was inserted into him as he was preparing to produce man. When man was produced, therefore, he was not composed of only two elements, body and soul, as the Demiurge had supposed, but of three: "the material, also called 'left,' which necessarily perishes since it cannot possibly receive the breath of imperishability; the psychic, also called 'right,' which lies between the spiritual and the material and extends to either one as it has the inclination; the spiritual, which was sent forth to be shaped in union with the psychic and to be instructed with it in its conduct." [4]

This does not mean that every individual human being has all three of these constituent elements within him. On the contrary, there are some men who are merely material or "fleshly," and they are banned forever from eternal life, since "flesh and blood cannot inherit the kingdom of God" (1 Corinthians 15:50). At the opposite extreme are the genuinely spiritual or "gnostic"—those possessing true knowledge—who "cannot damage or lose [their] spiritual nature, even if [they] engage in various material actions." [5] Between these two lie the psychic men, who can be saved if they obey the commandments but will be damned if they do not. These are members of the "earthly church," who cannot hope to attain to the ultimate fullness (*Plērōma*) but will, with the Demiurge, come to a middle place provided they practice sexual continence and good conduct.

When the history of the universe and of man was about to reach its consummation or completion, another emanation appeared. This radiation brought man the Word, who originated from the Ultimate and who was in the thought and the mind of the Father. The Word was the Savior, which was the name of what he was to do for the redemption of men.

Evidently there was a development in Gnostic speculation about this Savior between the statements of the *Gospel of Truth* and the Valentinian systems reported by the church fathers. In the latter systems the disjunction between the supreme God and the created, material world produced a picture of the Savior who assumed the spiritual and the psychic, but nothing of the material. He was not born physically, but only "passed through Mary as water passes through a pipe."[6] Nor could Christ die physically; therefore the Spirit of Christ departed from him when he was led before Pilate. (In another Gnostic system, that of Basilides, Simon of Cyrene [see Matthew 27:32] traded places with Jesus and was crucified in his stead.) After the crucifixion Christ raised the mortal (though not material) body of Jesus and transported it to the right hand of the Creator. Through Christ the elect receive the knowledge needed for their own ascent into the ultimate fullness, or *Plērōma*.

Now all of this has remained hidden from ordinary men—hidden, first of all, in the divine depths; but then hidden in the secret traditions of the Gnostic *elite*. The Savior explained it in parables so that only those would understand it who had the true knowledge (*gnōsis*). Such true knowledge is necessary for the understanding of the rest of the Bible. Since most of the members of the earthly church have not been inducted into these mysteries and are merely "psychic" rather than truly spiritual in their nature, they should hearken to the ultimate revelations conveyed through the true church of the Gnostics.

Anti-Gnostic Reactions

Any Christian who is acquainted with the New Testament will recognize in the foregoing many likenesses with its language and thought. It is especially the Gospel of John that the devotees of Valentinian Gnosticism found to their liking, much as Marcion laid claim to the Paul of Galatians. Despite these affinities, however, the orthodox fathers of the church charged both the Marcionites and the Valentinians with dangerous heresy. They cited many grounds for this charge, some of them obviously slanderous; but at least two are certainly accurate and fundamental enough to bear repetition here.

In its understanding of God, Gnosticism made a distinction between the Creator and the Redeemer. It then assigned the work of creation to a lesser divine being.

In its understanding of humanity, Gnosticism divided human beings into three types: the material, the psychic, and the spiritual. This division introduced the question of the Christian attitude toward inequality among men—not the inequality based upon prejudice, but the inherent inequality of ability and endowment.

Both our American and our Protestant heritage incline us to reject indignantly any system of thought that seems to make this inequality permanent or hierarchical. Or do they? Do Christians tolerate class structure? Should they? What about the Gnostic claim that the truly "spiritual"—that is, the truly Gnostic man—is above the moral and the doctrinal standards of ordinary Christians? Do similar claims exist in present-day experience?

No self-respecting Christian thought, whether in the first century or in the twentieth, can treat the doctrine of creation as negotiable. The implication of the doctrines of Marcion, Valentinus, and most other Gnostics was a disparagement of the created world and of man's createdness that the church fathers regarded as blasphemous, or irreverent. Neither the later doctrines of original sin nor the practices of Christian asceticism—practices of strict self-denial as a way of religious discipline—were ever permitted to blot out completely the affirmation of the goodness of created existence, which is the repeated refrain of the story of creation in the book of Genesis: "And God saw everything that he had made, and behold, it was very good" (Genesis 1:31).

Gnosticism identified creation with the fall into sin, and it sought to redeem man *from* his created physical existence rather than *in* it. No objection recurs more often in the writings of the anti-Gnostic fathers.

Apparently contradictory to this disparagement of created existence and of the body was the sexual license in which at least some
Gnostics seem to have indulged. "Just as gold placed in mud does
not lose its beauty but retains its own nature, and the mud cannot
harm the gold," Irenaeus quotes the Valentinians as boasting, "so we
cannot damage or lose our spiritual nature, even if we engage in
various material actions." [7]

Yet such license was consistent with the contempt of the Gnostics
toward the body. Being purely spiritual, they were above such
things as mere lust, and their self-indulgence could prove it; it
would also symbolize the pairings by which the heavenly aeons produced yet other aeons.

To the anti-Gnostic fathers all of this was proof—all too welcome
proof—that Gnosticism was an enemy both of sound morals and of
faithful doctrine. Nevertheless, as several of the succeeding chapters
will suggest, Gnosticism forced the fathers of the second and third
centuries to identify and define clearly the meaning and relevance
of the Christian gospel with greater force and clarity than they
might have done without so threatening a challenge.

Chapter Eight
JUSTIN MARTYR

Christianity and Judaism

CHRISTIAN THOUGHT has always had the obligation to address both the church and the world. The accounts in the fourteenth and the seventeenth chapters of the book of Acts suggest that one of the assignments which the spokesmen of Christianity have usually taken on themselves is that of defending and interpreting the Christian faith to the cultured among its despisers—the philosophers and other intellectuals of their age. As chapter ten will indicate, there have been repeated attempts in Christian history to deny the legitimacy of this apologetic assignment. From the second century to the twentieth, however, theologians have found the apologetic assignment impossible to escape.

The Apologists

Apologetics, a systematic defense against criticism from outside the faith, is really older than Christianity. Many of its materials and methods can be found in Philo of Alexandria, a Jewish contemporary of Jesus who worked out a restatement and defense of Judaism in the language of contemporary philosophy. Although Clement of Alexandria (see chapter eleven) seems to have been the first Christian apologist to make explicit use of Philo, the pattern of Jewish apologetics makes its appearance in Christian literature even earlier. Throughout most of the second century, Christian authors, writing chiefly in Greek, addressed apologies not only to the intellectuals in general, but especially to the Roman emperors. These defenses had the twofold purpose of refuting the pagan slanders against Christian doctrine and Christian morals and of presenting the case for Christianity on grounds of rationality and plausibility.

According to Eusebius, a certain "Quadratus dedicated and addressed a discourse [to the emperor Hadrian, who ruled from 117–138], which he had composed in defense of our religion, because certain wicked men were endeavoring to molest our people." [1] The apology of Quadratus is the oldest of which we have any mention. Eusebius reports that Aristides also composed one during the reign of Hadrian. Portions of this are still in existence, but they are apparently in garbled form.

Even the apologies that have survived, however, are not necessarily a reliable index to the full range of the thought of their authors. In efforts to find common ground with their Greek readers, they overemphasize certain points at the expense of others. This difference between the apologist's address to "the world" and his grasp of the full faith of the church has become evident with the discovery and publication of a sermon on the passion of Christ by Melito, another of the second-century apologists. Melito was bishop of Sardis, a city in the Roman province of Asia. Before this document came to light, Melito was known only as the author of an apology cited by Eusebius, in which the claim was made that the philosophy (Christianity) of these apologists had become a favorable boon to the Roman Empire. From this it would be possible to draw the conclusion that Melito and the other apologists held to "a philosophical religion which clothes Greek ideas and conceptions in a loose biblical garment, and which in the end issues in man's self-redemption ethically conceived." [2] However, now that we have access to the message addressed by an apologist to the church, we must be much more cautious before voicing such accusations.

A Christian in Philosopher's Garb

Of all the Greek apologists, the most important is Justin Martyr. Although very little information is available about his early life, he did incorporate a brief intellectual autobiography into the second chapter of one of his treatises, *The Dialogue with Trypho the Jew*. From the address of his *First Apology* we know that his father's name was Priscus and his grandfather's Bacchius, and that they were natives of Flavia Neapolis in Palestine (according to the Jewish historian, Josephus, the location of the biblical Shechem). He was evidently the child of a pagan home. His religious and intellectual development took him through a series of systems.

The first of Justin's philosophical masters was a Stoic,* from whom he tried to obtain knowledge about God. However, the teacher himself did not know God, and said that such instruction was unnecessary. From Stoicism, Justin turned to an itinerant philosopher, but quickly left him when instruction in philosophical truth was made conditional on the payment of a tuition fee.

The next stage of Justin's odyssey, or wandering, brought him to a self-satisfied Pythagorean—a member of the school of philosophy named after Pythagoras, sixth century B.C. Greek philosopher and mathematician. The Pythagorean asked him if he was acquainted with music, astronomy, and geometry, also whether he could expect to understand any of the things that lead to a happy life without a knowledge of these sciences.

Finally Justin took up the study of Platonic philosophy under the tutelage of one who had recently moved into his vicinity, a man of wisdom who held a high position among the Platonists. The Platonic conception of the superiority of spirit to matter and Plato's famous doctrine of ideas captivated Justin, and he remained a devotee of Platonic (or, to use the modern title, Middle Platonic) speculation for quite some time.

While on a walk by the seashore, where he enjoyed going for such speculation and contemplation, Justin chanced to meet an old man, who engaged him in a philosophical dialogue about the meaning and the limits of Platonic doctrine. Since neither Platonic nor Pythagorean philosophy could supply a satisfactory answer to the questions about the nature of the human soul and the constitution of the world, Justin's conversationalist pointed him instead to the prophets, whom he described as "men more ancient than all those who are esteemed philosophers, both righteous and beloved by God, who spoke by the Divine Spirit, and foretold events which would take place, and which are now taking place." [3] The testimony of the old man touched Justin's heart. "A flame was kindled in my soul; and a love of the prophets, and of those men who are friends of Christ, possessed me; and whilst revolving his words in my mind,

---

* Stoicism is a school of philosophy that originated about 300 B.C. Its founder was Zeno of Citium; but it was later developed and popularized by Seneca, Epictetus, and Marcus Aurelius. The Stoics contended that man should conform freely to natural law, that virtue is the highest good, and that wise men are free from passion—unperturbed by both joy and grief.

I found this philosophy alone to be safe and profitable." [4] This it was, he says, that made him a Christian, and in that sense a philosopher. Elsewhere Justin reports that while he was still delighting in Plato's doctrines, the courage of Christians when facing death made their beliefs seem more persuasive to him.

Thus Christianity made its appeal to Justin—and, as we shall see, *through* Justin as well—as the divinely revealed answer to the question of the philosophers. In the apt phrase of Eusebius, Justin "presented the divine word in the garb of a philosopher." [5] From Ephesus, where his conversion seems to have taken place, he traveled to Rome and became a teacher. This was during the reign of Emperor Antoninus Pius (A.D. 138–161). It was apparently during the emperorship of Marcus Aurelius, the son of Antoninus Pius, that the opposition of pagan philosophers and officials to Justin reached its climax with his execution, perhaps in A.D. 165. One of Justin's most bitter enemies was Crescens, a Cynic philosopher whom Justin had called a lover of "bravado and boasting."

Roman Emperor Marcus Aurelius, a Stoic concerned for moral strength of the empire. Ironically, Aurelius conducted no systematic persecution of the Christians; yet some of the most glorious Christian martyrdoms occurred during his reign.

50

The Two Apologies

According to Eusebius, Justin wrote two apologies in defense of Christianity, the first of them addressed to Antoninus Verus; that is, Marcus Aurelius. The manuscript tradition of Justin's works does contain two apologies attributed to him; but modern scholarship tends to believe that the so-called *Second Apology* is not the one to which Eusebius refers, which has probably been lost, but an appendix attached to the first and, like it, composed under Antoninus Pius. Many of the debating points scored by the other apologists appear in these two apologies, both in Justin's defense against pagan attacks and in his counterattacks.

One of the principal attacks on Christianity was the charge of atheism. As we have seen from *The Martyrdom of Polycarp*, the Roman mob called for the execution of the Christians with the cry: "Away with the atheists!" Closely coupled with this charge was the accusation of sedition, or resistance to official governmental authority. In fact, "atheism" did not mean chiefly a philosophical or theological doctrine, but a form of social and political nonconformity—the refusal to perform the duties of acknowledging and worshiping the public deities, including the Roman emperor himself, who by this time was being credited with many of the attributes of divinity. A modern analogy would be the refusal of certain religious groups to salute or pledge allegiance to the flag. Justin willingly acknowledged: "We confess that we are atheists, so far as the gods of this sort are concerned, but not with respect to the most true God, the Father of righteousness and temperance and the other virtues, who is free from all impurity." [6]

In their recognition of the counterfeit character of the pagan deities, however, the Christians were following the example of the noblest spirits of antiquity, especially of Socrates, who had also been accused of atheism by the adherents of false gods. Thus the Christians, like Socrates, had incurred the wrath of demons, who were now plotting against them. In response to the charge of disloyalty, Justin cited the words of Jesus: "Render . . . to Caesar the things that are Caesar's, and to God the things that are God's" (Matthew 22:21). Therefore worship belonged to God, and properly to him alone; but in every other way the Christians were happy to yield to Caesar every expression of loyalty and service.

When the apologists turned from the criticisms of their opponents to the positive arguments in support of Christianity, one of their favorites was often the antiquity of the Christian writings. Thus Justin declares that the doctrines "we assert in conformity with what has been taught us by Christ, and by the prophets who preceded him, are alone true, and are older than all the writers who have existed." [7] This argument from antiquity is elaborated in a series of comments on the prophecies of the Old Testament, all calculated to prove that various details of the birth, life, death, and resurrection of Jesus Christ had been foretold by the prophets. Anyone who is impartial in his judgment, according to Justin, will have to concede that this correspondence between Old Testament prediction and New Testament history is sufficient to produce conviction and belief in those who embrace truth, are not bigoted in their opinions, and are not governed by passion. Yet this reliance on the Old Testament must not be permitted to conceal Justin's willingness to find support for his position in parallels between biblical history and the myths and symbols of Greece and Rome. Even Plato drew his doctrine of creation from Moses—a claim that is repeated by many of the apologists and that had already been put forth by Philo.

Another argument in support of Christianity was its moral superiority as demonstrated in its effects on believers. As we have seen, Justin claimed that the steadfastness of Christians when confronted by peril had impressed him while he was still a pagan. Pointing to the examples of members of the church, he contrasted pagan and Christian morals. There were many Christians, not only women but even men, who had remained chaste throughout a lifetime of sixty or seventy years. There were others whom Christianity had led to reform their intemperate habits and to put off their immoral ways, for Christ had come to call not the righteous but the sinners. Thus the accusations against the Christians were slanders, for by their moral uprightness and their obedience to the commands of Christ they were an asset and a support to the life of the empire. Others may have obeyed the imperial laws through fear of punishment by the emperor, but Christians "more than all other men are [the emperor's] helpers and allies in promoting peace, seeing that we hold this view, that it is alike impossible for the wicked, the covetous, the conspirator, and for the virtuous, to escape the notice of God, and that each man goes to everlasting punishment or salvation according to the value of his actions."[8] Even simple justice required, therefore, that the early Christians receive a fair hearing and not be condemned out of hand merely for bearing the hated name.

The Dialogue with Trypho

Justin Martyr is a crucial figure in the history of early Christianity, not only because his two apologies addressed to the emperor are the most important of the early defenses of Christianity against paganism still in existence (at least until Origen's *Against Celsus,* to be discussed in chapter twelve), but also because he is the author of the earliest and most notable of the many Christian defenses of Christianity against Judaism, *The Dialogue with Trypho the Jew.* From the first chapters of Paul's Epistle to the Romans we know that the early church was doing battle simultaneously on two fronts, that against paganism and that against Judaism; but only with Justin do we begin to see the shift in the relative significance of these two fronts as the spokesmen for Christianity come from a pagan rather than from a Jewish background. *The Dialogue with Trypho* is the oldest treatise we have of this sizable literature on Christianity and Judaism. It is also the most balanced for centuries to come; in fact, "there is no dialogue as such which is conducted on quite so high a level of courteousness and fairness until . . . the end of the eleventh century."[9]

In form, *The Dialogue with Trypho* is supposed to be the account of a conversation held about A.D. 136 between Justin and "Trypho," which may be Justin's way of describing the distinguished Rabbi Tarphon, although it seems almost certain that this was not his partner in the actual debate. *The Dialogue* was not written down until twenty years or so later, and is by no means a word-for-word transcript of the discussion; nor is it, however, merely a literary device, for Trypho argues much more effectively than he would in a dialogue that was completely "rigged" by a Christian author. The Christian case in relation to the claims of Judaism is summarized here in a book that contains many of the points which were to become stock arguments for centuries. Three of these constitute the basic outline of the book.

A large section of *The Dialogue* is given over to Justin's refutation of Trypho's charge that the Christians, professing to be pious and

THE MIRACULOUS WELL OF MIRIAM, *depicting Moses distributing water to the twelve tribes of Israel—symbolizing the nourishing of the tribes. The mural was found at Dura-Europos, ancient city on the Euphrates between Aleppo and Baghdad—abandoned by the Romans in A.D. 256.*

supposing themselves better than others, are not in any particular way different from the Jews; specifically, by the observance of the law of Moses. This charge, according to Justin, rests on a superficial understanding of the law of Moses itself. For this law was not meant to be permanently binding, but pointed beyond itself to the time when it would be fulfilled and thus set aside and replaced. Fasting, circumcision, sacrifices, and the like all had a symbolic importance until the coming of the Messiah, but now the symbols have given way to the reality of that which they predicted. Even the Old Testament Scriptures are also believed by the Christians, and various passages in the book of Psalms are used to prove that Jesus Christ is the one to whose coming the saints of Israel looked with expectation.

The defense of the Christian view of Jesus Christ is a second major issue of *The Dialogue*. Trypho finds it especially hard to understand why there had to be two comings of Christ, one in humility and suffering and the other in glory for judgment. Justin marshals arguments from Old Testament prophecy to demonstrate that the twofold advent of the Messiah had been predicted long before. From the same source he proves, as he also had in the *First Apology*, that specific events in the life of Jesus, from the virgin birth to the resurrection, had been announced beforehand by the patriarchs and prophets. But for Trypho the most troubling feature of the Christian estimate of Christ is the habit of calling him "God." In defense of this practice Justin cites various Old Testament revelations of the deity such as the appearances to Abraham, to Jacob, and to Moses, in all of which he who appeared "is called God [and yet] is distinct from him who made all things—numerically, I mean, not [distinct] in will." [10] These and other passages from the Old Testament show that Christ is truly God and deserves to be worshiped as such; they show it so clearly that the Jews have taken it upon themselves not only to distort the interpretation of the Old Testament but even to mutilate, or alter, its text.

By their rejection of Christ, therefore, the Jews had forfeited the right to be called "the people of God." Now it was the Christians who had become the chosen people and the true sons of Abraham; "all who through [Jesus Christ] have fled for refuge to the Father constitute the blessed Israel," or, as Justin says later on, "the true Israelitic race." [11] Among the indications in the Old Testament that the Law and the covenant were to pass were the prophecies that the Gentiles would be converted. That had now begun to happen, but through Christianity. This did not mean that the Jews are excluded permanently from salvation, but that it becomes available to them only as it does to the Gentiles; namely, through Christ.

Both to the Gentiles and to the Jews, therefore, Justin addressed an appeal that acknowledged the temporary and partial validity of the insights granted to them, but that invited them to the fullness now disclosed in Christ, in whom the schism between Jew and Gentile was healed and the salvation of all men was made manifest.

Chapter Nine
IRENAEUS OF LYONS

The Question of Authority

OF THE MANY THOUSANDS of Christians who lived during the first three centuries after Christ, the names of only a few hundred have come down to us, and of these far fewer than a hundred wrote anything that still exists. Therefore the writings of the early fathers of the church are the voice of a tiny minority of the early Christian community.

This situation compels us to ask, in the jargon of the public opinion polls, just how reliable a "sampling" of Christian belief and practice we can obtain from these writings. In our own day it certainly would not do to generalize about the beliefs of church members on the basis of the opinions of the clergy, and yet most of the authors being studied here were clergy. There is, of course, no way to prove the claim of these authors that they are speaking in the name of the entire Christian community. Nevertheless, one criterion has already been suggested by the discussion in chapter six. Some Christian teachers professed to derive their understandings and their teachings from a secret tradition that was unavailable to the ordinary believer in the ranks.

Other Christians appealed to the common mind of the church and to its public tradition as proof of their teaching. It does seem reasonable to argue that they would not have dared to make such an appeal in support of notions that did not have at least some general acceptance. The problem of what is normative, or authoritative, in Christian teaching was thus central to the life and unity of the church—then as now. Authority seldom receives intensive and extensive consideration; but when it does, it is seen as one of the major issues in contemporary life.

The Peacemaker

No church father addressed that problem more directly than Irenaeus of Lyons. Neither the date of his birth nor the date of his death can be determined with any precision. He seems to have been born in Asia Minor, perhaps in Smyrna; for we have already quoted at length from a letter in which Irenaeus reminisces about his youth in Asia Minor, where he claims to have listened eagerly to the teaching of Polycarp. Since Polycarp in turn claimed to have listened to the teaching of the apostles, this made Irenaeus the spiritual grandson of the apostle John. This background as the direct heir of the apostolic tradition may help to explain why Irenaeus made such a point of apostolic legitimacy as the norm of Christian teaching and practice. "Only one intervening generation of tradition separated its author [Irenaeus] from the apostles themselves, and its [his *Proof of the Apostolic Preaching*] value lies in the fact that, invested as it is with the authority of so early a successor to the apostolic ministry, it is the earliest document we have that professes to give an exposition of the basis on which the apostolic preaching rests." [1]

From his childhood home in Asia Minor, Irenaeus went to Gaul, which by this time was no longer divided into three parts but was in the process of becoming Romanized. In the church at Lugdunum, the modern Lyons, Irenaeus served as presbyter, and presumably he was ordained there. During the decade following A.D. 170, the church there was seriously troubled by the Montanist sect (Montanism is discussed in chapter ten) and dispatched Irenaeus to Rome to consult with the bishop of Rome, Eleutherus. Upon his return to Lyons, Irenaeus found the church deprived of its bishop,

MARBURG — ART REFERENCE BUREAU

A fourth-century sarcophagus showing Christ sending forth the twelve apostles.

Pothinus, who had been martyred at the age of ninety. Irenaeus was chosen as his successor. The role of mediator which he had assumed during the Montanist crisis was thrust upon him again some years later, when he sought to reconcile Victor, the bishop of Rome, and the bishops of Asia Minor whom Victor had excommunicated in a controversy about the date of Easter. As Eusebius observes, Irenaeus was "a man well-named, for he was a peacemaker both in name [the Greek word *eirenaios* means "peaceable"] and character." [2]

Unfortunately, the chief writing for which Irenaeus is noted does not make him seem much of a peacemaker. Usually called *Against the Heresies,* it is one of the principal sources for our knowledge of Marcion, Valentinus, and other Gnostics—whom Irenaeus cites and refutes at great length in his treatise. Until our own century this was the only writing of Irenaeus in existence, except for some fragments. In 1904, however, there was discovered the manuscript of a sixth-century Armenian translation of a book of Irenaeus previously known only by its title, *The Proof of the Apostolic Preaching,* which has been edited, translated, and published several times. We know from Eusebius and from other writers that Irenaeus wrote other books as well, but only fragments have survived. Eusebius makes no mention of his death, and the tradition that he died a martyr is both late and unreliable. Once again, it is the career and the thought of a church father, rather than his biography, that must claim our attention.

The Problem of Authority

Both the Montanists on whose behalf Irenaeus interceded with Eleutherus and the Gnostics against whom he directed his *Against the Heresies* had raised the problem of authority, the former by laying claim to private revelations and the latter by claiming to possess secret traditions that were unavailable to the rank and file of Christians. It was particularly in reaction to the Gnostic threat that Irenaeus worked out his definition of the faith which "the church, though dispersed throughout the whole world, even to the ends of the earth, has received from the apostles and their disciples." [3] The Gnostics dismissed this universal and "catholic" faith as suitable only for the "psychics" of the church (persons especially sensitive to supernatural forces) but as quite inadequate for the truly "spiritual" Gnostics. Had not the apostle Paul said (1 Corinthians 2:15),

"The spiritual man judges all things, but is himself to be judged by no one"? The Gnostics took this to mean that the Gnostic elite could not be judged by the same norms that applied to the rank and file of the church. Irenaeus, on the other hand, insisted that the same passage applies only to those who read the Scriptures carefully along with the presbyters in the church, among whom the apostolic doctrine is found.

The problem of authority was made more acute by the language of much of the New Testament. Setting himself against the religious establishment of his people, Jesus had contrasted what "was said to the men of old" (Matthew 5:21; 5:33) with what he said on his own authority. The opponents of Irenaeus took this to involve opposition to and the overturning of the teachings and principles of the past. The language of the Gospels, like that of the prophets, was more explicit in its rejection of false traditions than in its assertion of continuity with tradition. Even when the Gospels speak of Christ as the fulfillment of Old Testament prophecy, this is as much an attack upon the Jews for failing to recognize this fact as it is a positive assertion. In the hands of the Gnostics this accent of the New Testament could be turned into a justification for their idea of a secret tradition—above and beyond the public memoirs of the apostles as read and interpreted in the Christian community.

It was only with the book of Acts and with the Pastoral Epistles—1 and 2 Timothy, and Titus—that the writers of the New Testament addressed themselves to the question of the continuing authority in the church after the passing of those who had known and heard the Lord personally. It is significant both that some of the Gnostic groups rejected the book of Acts and that the "myths and genealogies" against which the pastoral epistles warn might very likely be Gnostic accounts of the beginning of the universe. When Irenaeus took up the task of answering the Gnostics in the name of apostolic orthodoxy, therefore, both the internal development and the controversies of the church had brought the question of continuing authority in the church to the point where a fuller and clearer definition of authority was a matter of utmost necessity.

The Apostolic Tradition

As we have already noted, Irenaeus had reason to be very conscious of standing in the direct succession of the apostles. What is more,

THE TRINITY IN GLORY, *a fifteenth-century painting depicting Mary enthroned to the left of the three figures representing the Trinity, and a photo of a rabbi ministering to an injured civil rights demonstrator.*

this was not simply a projection of his own personal experience and situation as a pupil of the pupil of the apostles. Such a theory of authority would have played right into the hand of the Gnostics, whose idea of tradition was in some ways a special version of the widespread Near Eastern notion that a "seventh son of a seventh son" had access to the deepest secrets. On the contrary, Irenaeus claimed this authority not for himself but for the church, "since the apostles, like a rich man [depositing his money] in a bank, lodged in her hands most copiously all things pertaining to the truth; so that every man, whosoever will, can draw from her the water of life." [4] The answer and the antidote to the secret traditions of the Gnostics is the authority of the apostolic tradition.

Where is this tradition to be found, and how is it to be verified? The answer of Irenaeus may appear at first to be an argument in a circle. On the one hand, he appealed to the authority of "the gospel . . . by the will of God handed down to us in the Scriptures to be the ground and pillar of our faith." [5] In the next breath, when pressed by his opponents, he cited "those who were by the apostles instituted bishops in the churches, and [demonstrated] the succession of these men to our own times." [6] As the outstanding example of this succession he pointed to the church at Rome, adding that "it is a matter of necessity that every church should agree with this church, on account of its preeminent authority." [7] Anyone who approaches Irenaeus with a mental set determined by the theological controversies of the Reformation will find him thoroughly confusing, for in his doctrine of authority Irenaeus refused to choose *between* the Bible and tradition.

To make sense of Irenaeus, it is necessary to disengage ourselves from the antitheses, or contradictory opinions, of the Reformation period and to identify the seat of religious authority—short of the authority of Christ himself—in the apostles, who were chosen and commissioned by Christ. To them he handed down—"traditioned," to employ a rare but useful English verb—the word and will of God. Initially, of course, this was communicated orally, through preaching; but eventually the apostles had to set down the word of God in a written form. This does not mean that there was no written form of the word of God before the composition of the Gospels and epistles, for the apostles still had the Old Testament and used portions of it (as Irenaeus himself did in his *Proof of the Apostolic*

Preaching) as the authority for their message. The Old Testament and the collection of apostolic writings together constituted the norm of apostolic Christianity for Irenaeus. It is still too early to speak of a "New Testament canon."

Nevertheless, the apostles were not merely bookmen according to Irenaeus; nor was the church a sacred library. The same apostles who set down the traditions of the Lord also founded churches, to which they handed down (traditioned) the correct way of interpreting the Scriptures. To these churches and their episcopal sees * one was to look for authentic apostolic tradition. "Since, therefore, the tradition from the apostles does thus exist in the church, and is permanent among us, let us revert to the scriptural proof furnished by those apostles who did also write the gospel." [8] Apostolic tradition would, then, appear to include three distinct parts that have often been set into opposition in later centuries: the Scriptures of the Old and New Testaments; the doctrinal confession and creed of the church, together with the proper method of biblical interpretation; and the witness of the continuing magisterium or teaching power of the church, as embodied in the apostolic sees, of which Rome is the preeminent one.

Irenaeus does not seem to have considered the possibility that these three entities would ever come into conflict, or that any one of them could be isolated from the others and elevated as the sole authority. Whatever may be the conclusions one draws from this for later debates, it is essential above all that one measure the full scope of what Irenaeus and those who followed him meant by the authority of the apostolic tradition.

The First and the Second Adam

The weight of the apostolic tradition and the challenge of the Gnostic heretics caused Irenaeus to discuss many of the great themes of Christian doctrine—such as the meaning of creation, the work of the Holy Spirit, the relation between the old and the new covenant, and the second coming of Christ. As chapter six has indicated, however, one of the principal objects of the Gnostic challenge was the Chris-

---

* Sometimes the word "see" refers to the seat of authority, or the center of power, of a bishop—the diocesan center. At other times it refers to the territory of jurisdiction (such as a diocese, or province) of a bishop.

An American Legion commander, a veteran of the Korean campaign, marches in an anti-war demonstration. The question of authority is a recurring issue in human experience.

tian understanding of the salvation achieved by Christ. Not surprisingly, therefore, one of the chief theological accomplishments for which Irenaeus is remembered was his detailed account of the work of Christ as the restoration of fallen humanity.

The coming of Christ was necessary not, as the Gnostics argued, because of an inadequacy in the work of the Creator, but because man, God's pure creature, disobeyed the command of God, and disobedience to God results in death. The word "pure" applies to Adam rather than the word "perfect," for Adam and Eve were naïve as children in their dreaming innocence. After being seduced by the devil into sin, they became debtors to death. Instead of growing from innocent purity toward perfection, as had been intended by the Creator, they allowed themselves to become captives to the power of Satan. "Communion with God is life and light, and the enjoyment of all the benefits which he has in store. . . . But separation from God is death, and separation from light is darkness; and separation from God consists in the loss of all the benefits which he has in store." [9] Thus the consequences of man's disobedience are both moral (sin) and physical (death), and he cannot set himself free of either.

What man cannot do of himself and for himself, God in Christ does for him. To liberate from sin and death a humanity that consists of flesh and blood, the Savior himself must take on flesh and blood. This cannot be imaginary, as the Gnostics contend, for a fictitious incarnation could not achieve the real salvation of men with real bodies. The term that Irenaeus employs for this work of incarnation and salvation is "recapitulation." Reference to the work of recapitulation appears also in the New Testament (see Ephesians 1:10). Irenaeus may have borrowed ideas concerning this work from Justin Martyr. Recapitulation is the achievement of salvation through the life, death, and resurrection of Christ, the Second Adam. It was the work of God himself; for "the Father is that which is invisible about the Son, but the Son is that which is visible about the Father." [10]

Having entered human history in the incarnation, God in Christ "recapitulates" the stages of human life through which the First Adam has passed; but he brings victory in place of the disobedience, defeat, and death that marked the path of the First Adam through this world. "So the Word was made flesh, in order that sin, destroyed by means of that same flesh through which it had gained the mastery and taken hold and lorded it, should no longer be in us." [11] Irenaeus went so far as to maintain that Christ had actually lived to an age of forty or fifty. "He passed through every age, becoming an infant for infants . . . a child for children . . . a youth for youths . . . an old man for old men, that he might be a perfect Master for all" and participate in all the phases of a truly human existence.[12]

The obedience of Christ undoes the damage of Adam's disobedience; his death and resurrection bring release from the death caused by Adam's sin. Thus Christ is the Second Adam, through whom, as the apostle Paul had said, "as one man's trespass led to condemnation for all men, so one man's act of righteousness leads to acquittal and life for all men" (Romans 5:18). By his formulation of this account of the reconciliation achieved in Christ, Irenaeus laid down a pattern that was to be worked out in greater detail and with greater care by later church fathers such as Athanasius (see chapter sixteen).

Nevertheless, it is a mistake to attribute to Irenaeus a theory of the atonement in the sense of the later conceptions of the medieval theologian Anselm or the American theologian Horace Bushnell. The intent of Irenaeus is much less technical, more practical. He was intent upon making clear the apostolic tradition, and defending it against the distortions and attacks of the Gnostics. In the performance of this task, he had to declare forcefully that the man Jesus Christ was no horrible fabrication but flesh of our flesh and bone of our bone, who participated in the real history of our humanity. Because the reality of all of this was as offensive to the Gnostics as it has sometimes been to Christians who have claimed to be orthodox, he reinforced it with his doctrine of recapitulation. Thus he helped to fortify a central Christian affirmation without which there would be no gospel and no church.

*The bottom of a marriage bowl
dating from the fourth century,
and a contemporary drawing of
a young woman.*

JACKI BERNI

Chapter Ten
TERTULLIAN OF CARTHAGE

Discipline in Freedom

THE FACT THAT Christianity makes people more moral and law-abiding is commonly assumed. The evidence in support of this claim is not as convincing as it might be, however. As soon as one concerns himself with the issue of morality, he confronts one of the most perplexing questions of human existence: What *is* morality? This question throws one into the consideration of the role of discipline. Yet Christianity also stresses freedom. The question therefore becomes even more complex—and more basic: What is the role of discipline in freedom? In what manner and to what degree are accountability and responsibility involved?

We have had repeated occasion to note how scant is our information about the lives and careers of most of the early fathers of the church. We know somewhat more, however, about the man with whom we deal in this chapter—Tertullian of Carthage. Unfortunately, much of what we know we do not like, for Tertullian stood for ethical rigorism. Strenuously, and with great passion, he called for discipline. Such discipline and self-denial applied to all the areas of the ethical life, maintained Tertullian; but to none of these areas did he apply it more intensely than to the ethics of sex. He was remembered by later generations for his violent attacks on remarriage.

In reflecting upon Tertullian's plea for rigorous discipline, it will be important to bear in mind that the complex issue of the proper mixture of freedom and discipline is still very much with us in the middle of the twentieth century. Perhaps this is nowhere more evident than in the following statements from a recent book on the subject.

Young people rebuild a burned church in
Ripley, Mississippi.

No person, no society, can continue or cohere for any length of time
without an accepted ethic, just as ordered life becomes impossible
without a recognized legal system or a stable economy. And the Christian least of all can be disinterested in these fields. The more he loves
his neighbor, the more he will be concerned that the whole *ethos*
[character or tone] of his society—cultural, moral, legal, political and
economic—is a good one, preserving personality rather than destroying it.

But he will also be the first to confess that Christ does not supply
him with an ethical code, any more than he supplies him with a legal
system, or a polity, or an economy. For it was not Jesus' purpose to
provide any of these. Jesus' purpose was to call men to the kingdom of
God, to subject everything in their lives to the overriding, unconditional claim of God's utterly gracious yet utterly demanding rule of
righteous love. And men could not acknowledge this claim without
accepting the constraint of the same sacrificial, unself-regarding *agape*
[self-giving love] over all their relations with each other. It is this
undeviating claim, this inescapable constraint, which provides the
profoundly constant element in the distinctively Christian response in
every age or clime. For it produces in Christians, however different
or diversely placed, a direction, a cast, a style of life, which is recognizably and gloriously the same. Yet *what* precisely they must do to
embody this claim will differ with every century, group and individual.[1]

Tertullian was an opponent who argued a great deal, a Christian materialist whose belief in a physical hell has been called "a vision of the disordered imagination without parallel except, perhaps, among his spiritual descendants, the New England Puritans." [2] He was also an anti-intellectual who is remembered for having said, "I believe because it is absurd." (Although he apparently did not say these exact words, there are statements to approximately this effect in his writings.)

Yet this conventional picture of Tertullian is something of a caricature, for a scholar of the stature of Father Quasten has judged that "except for St. Augustine, Tertullian is the most important and original ecclesiastical author in Latin," [3] more important than even Ambrose or Jerome.

The text of the Roman law (*Corpus Juris Civilis*) contains several references to a jurist named "Tertullianus." Although historians a generation ago questioned the identification of this jurist with the church father Tertullian, it seems more reasonable today. His treatise, *The Prescriptions Against the Heretics*, has been shown to bear marks of a legal and rhetorical training. Tertullian's father was a centurion in Carthage and was a pagan, as was Tertullian's mother. The date of his birth appears to be about A.D. 155, but he did not become a Christian until sometime in the 190's. According to Jerome, he also became a priest, but this cannot be established from his writings.

Tertullian was married and, as we shall see, addressed one of his writings to his wife. He was eventually drawn to the Montanist movement and joined what we might call the first sect about 207. The year of his death should probably be placed at approximately A.D. 220. He left behind a large body of writings, thirty-one in all, written in Latin. Other works, some of them in Greek, have been lost. For our purposes here, his most important works are those dealing with the discipline of the Christian life and with the related issues of the Montanist controversy.

The Montanist Sect

Although Tertullian is by far the best-known of the adherents of the Montanist sect, he was in fact a member of its second generation. The movement began in Phrygia during the second half of the second century, when Montanus, "a recent convert to the faith

... suddenly fell into a state of possession, as it were, and abnormal ecstasy," [4] prophesying, among other things, that the end of history was at hand and that the heavenly Jerusalem would soon descend near Pepuza, a small town in Phrygia. In this message he was joined by two prophetesses, Priscilla and Maximilla. As the so-called new prophecy developed, Montanus came to be regarded—either by himself or, more probably, by his later followers—as the fulfillment of the promises of the Counselor ("Paraclete") given in passages such as John 14:15-17, 26; 15:26; 16:7-14. With this announcement of the imminent end of all things seems to have been joined at least some denunciation of the church, and especially of its leaders, for undue conformity to the world.

In the form it acquired at the hands of Tertullian, Montanism came to make this denunciation of the secularization of the church a central tenet, basing upon it a summons to penitence and to a revival of the strict and rigorous discipline that had been lost through compromise.

The Denial of the World

Tertullian is peculiarly the preacher of Christian discipline. Despite his attack on *The Shepherd* as the only scripture that is favorable to adulterers, there is a recognizable resemblance between him and Hermas, whose thought about discipline we studied in chapter five. However, almost a century separates the two men—a century during which many Christians suffered martyrdom but during which the church also grew in size and prestige.

Tertullian called for a rededication to the loyalties of the apostolic age and for Christian heroism under suffering. He wrote: "If you have to lay down your life for God, it is not in gentle fevers and on soft beds, but in the sharp pains of martyrdom: you must take up the cross and bear it after your Master, as he has himself instructed you [see Matthew 16:24]. The sole key to unlock Paradise is your own life's blood." [5] With bitter scorn Tertullian attacked the self-indulgence of the pagans and (in his Montanist period) the high living of professed Christians.

Behind this preoccupation with discipline and self-denial lies the risk involved in the Christian gospel of the forgiveness of sins and justification by grace through faith. In his epistles to the Romans and to the Galatians, the apostle Paul had felt it necessary

What is freedom?

to insist that the gift of salvation in Christ did not confer on believers a license to sin or to expect an affirmative answer to the question: "Are we to continue in sin that grace may abound?" (Romans 6:1). The Epistle of James was apparently addressed to an audience where just such a conclusion was in vogue. It argued that without the discipline of good works, faith is dead. We have seen that Christians in the second century were troubled by the question of forgiveness for sins committed after baptism, but the Epistle to the Hebrews had already declared that "it is impossible to restore again to repentance those who have once been enlightened [which may mean 'baptized'], who have tasted the heavenly gift, and have become partakers of the Holy Spirit . . . if they then commit apostasy" (Hebrews 6:4–6).

71

The lists of the sins that could and could not be forgiven after baptism varied greatly from one church father to another, and presumably also from one church to another. However, as the members of the church felt less urgency—if only slightly less—about the return of Christ and about the denial of the world, the problem of discipline inevitably became a thorny one. It was to remain so throughout the third century.

The Discipline of Penitence

In the history of Christian ethics Tertullian is ordinarily designated a "rigorist"—one who demanded adherence to the letter of the law and who refused to make concessions to the frailty of the flesh. So consistent was his rigorism that even today it is difficult to determine whether certain of his treatises date from the time of his allegiance to the ascetic ethic of the Montanist sect or from an earlier period when, though not yet a Montanist, he was already urging Christians to practice the discipline of penitence. Tertullian could therefore pray, both as a Catholic and then as a Montanist: "Grant, Lord Christ, that thy servants may speak of the discipline of penitence, or hear of it, only while the duty of avoiding sin rests on them as catechumens [converts to Christianity receiving instruction in doctrine]. In other words, may they, thereafter, know nothing of repentance nor have any need of it." [6]

Tertullian dealt throughout his career with the problem of bigamy —not of bigamy in parallel, which all Christians condemned, but of what he called bigamy in series. He was remembered by later generations for his violent attacks on remarriage. Augustine, for example, speaks of "Tertullian, inflated with cheeks full of sound not of wisdom, whilst with railing tooth he attacks second marriages, as though unlawful, which the apostle with sober mind allows to be altogether lawful." [7] In fact, the evolution of his rigoristic attitude toward this question is a useful index of his movement from Catholic orthodoxy toward Montanist sectarianism, of which we shall be speaking later in this chapter. A brief explanation of his three treatises on the subject will introduce us to the working of his mind.

The first and best of the three treatises, written in two books, is entitled *To His Wife*, usually dated between A.D. 200 and 206. Its purpose was to discuss "the manner of life that ought to be yours after my departure from this world, should I be called before you." [8]

Book One sets forth the considerations that should deter Tertullian's wife from contracting a second marriage, which can be summarized as follows: (1) Marriage is good, but continence is better. (2) The polygamy practiced by the patriarchs is no argument in favor of multiple marriage. (3) The apostle Paul clearly shows his disapproval of second marriage. (4) It is lust, shown in a variety of ways, which causes people to marry a second time—and Christians should resist this desire. (5) The example of the saints encourages us to lead a life of self-restraint. (6) Even some pagans esteem and practice chastity. (7) When God separates husband and wife by the death of one or the other, he indicates that it is his will for them to remain single. (8) The church is against remarriage, and makes this clear by not admitting bigamists to the governing body of the church.

Book Two is a statement of the case against a religiously mixed marriage if Tertullian's wife should decide to marry a second time despite his counsel. It contrasts "the marriage of two Christians, two who are one in hope, one in desire, one in the way of life they follow, one in the religion they practice," [9] with a marriage between a Christian and a pagan, who cannot share the deepest experiences of life in God. Even if the pagan husband tolerates his wife's Christianity, such a marriage can harm her Christian faith.

The two later works on marriage and remarriage both show marks of Montanist ideas, even though one, *An Exhortation to Chastity*, was written before Tertullian's public acceptance of Montanism. It is addressed to a fellow Christian whose wife had recently died, and it counsels him against remarriage on the basis of many of the arguments given above. There is, however, a noticeable shift in Tertullian's attitude toward marriage as such. "Marriage and fornication are different," he writes, "only because laws appear to make them so; they are not intrinsically different, but only in the degree of their illegitimacy." [10]

Finally, the treatise entitled *Monogamy* is a Montanist tract through and through, advancing the arguments of the earlier books on the basis of the special revelations granted to the Montanists, and denouncing the church for its compromise with moral evil. As we turn now to the Montanist crisis, we can put Tertullian's bitter denunciations into the context of the struggle of the third-century church about the relation between the sacred and the secular.

GUNDA HOLZMEISTER FROM BILDER AUS ANATOLIEN

FRANK KOSTYU

Monastic cells hollowed out of volcanic rock, and experimental forms of Christian ministry—dramatizing opposite schools of thought regarding how Christians relate to the world. What is involved in secularization and secularism? When are Christians in the world and not of it? When are they of the world and not in it?

Secularization in the Church

The relation between the sacred and the secular, which has been a problem to Christians from the beginning, acquired new complexity as the church began to come to terms with the world and to reckon with the possibility that the second coming of Christ and the end of history, for which Christians prayed, might be postponed for quite a long time. Whether because of this factor or for some other reason, there is some ground for believing that the fervor of Christians had cooled by the end of the second century.

In the New Testament there are several instances of direct revelations from God in the form of visions or dreams. Although the orthodox writers of the church during the second and third centuries did not deny such revelations and sometimes even made the claim that they continued to come, it seems evident that private revelations and prophecies were declining, as well they might be expected to in a church that was developing structures of authority such as those which were discussed in chapter nine.

The practical concerns and requirements of church administration were also responsible for certain modifications in the discipline of the church. For example, Callistus, the bishop of Rome (who died about A.D. 223), was accused by Hippolytus of permitting adulterers and fornicators to return to the communion after a certain period of penitence.

All of these tendencies called forth a violent reaction from Tertullian—so violent that one is inclined to share the opinion of Ronald Knox that "behind all the fireworks there is no real substance in Tertullian's grievance against the church about its laxity of discipline. Secretly, you feel, he was grateful to the church for being lax, because Montanism was thereby enabled to go one better, and achieve a reputation for severity." [11]

Certainly it would be a mistake to equate the situation of the church at the end of the second century with that which was to prevail at the end of the fourth century, when the official acceptance of Christianity by the emperor and the empire turned the gospel into something socially acceptable and thus made it easier to be a Christian than not to be one. The growth of monasticism in that context is an indication that broad masses of church members were no longer as serious or as committed as Christians once had been.

Attitudes in a Redeeming Community

As we have already seen, Tertullian the Montanist intensified his misgivings about second marriage into outright prohibition, which, according to the Montanists, was now being revealed through the Paraclete, or Counselor.

In a treatise *On Fasting*, written near the end of his career, Tertullian defined the differences between the Montanists and the Catholics (whom he labels "the Psychics," as distinguished from "the Spirituals") in an epigram: "It is on this account that the New Prophecies are rejected . . . that they plainly teach more frequent fasting than marrying";[12] that is, that they prohibited remarriage but enjoined a much more severe discipline of fasting than that current in the church.

Yet another accusation against the Catholics, particularly against their clergy, was cowardice. Tertullian devoted a special essay to this issue, *Concerning Flight in Persecution*, where he warned: "If any one recognizes the Spirit also [that is, the voice of the Counselor], he will hear him branding the runaways." [13]

The most violent of Tertullian's Montanist denunciations of the church is probably the treatise *On Purity*. It took up the question of penitence after baptism, of which we have spoken earlier. As we have seen, the Roman bishop Callistus had adopted the practice of remitting even the sins of adultery and fornication under certain conditions, and he was certainly not the only one to do so. It cannot be determined, therefore, whether Callistus is the specific object of the bitter discussion in this treatise when Tertullian speaks of "a most faithful advocate . . . of adulterers, fornicators, and the incestuous, since it is to honor such as these that he has taken up this case against the Holy Spirit." [14] Not only did the precedent of Christ and the apostles not sanction such a policy in cases of penitential discipline, but the Montanist could claim: "I have the Paraclete himself saying in the person of the new prophets: 'The church can forgive sin, but I will not do it lest others also sin.'" [15] Thus the lateness of the hour in history demanded that the discipline of the church be tightened rather than relaxed.

It is noteworthy that, whatever other deviations in the movement there may have been, Tertullian the Montanist did not stray from the path of doctrinal orthodoxy (the official church formulation of truth) even when he forsook the external fellowship of the church Catholic. In fact, he argued for the correctness of the new prophecy on this very ground, that it had not brought about any defection from true doctrine. The Paraclete, or Counselor, had come to establish discipline, not to reveal or to proclaim new doctrine. Therefore, even though Tertullian's long treatise *Against Marcion* bears some traces of having been written, at least in its final form, during the author's Montanist period, it is by no means a statement of the opinions peculiar to that party, but summarizes the teaching and tradition of the church in a form that could be, and was, shared by those who repudiated the Montanist sect.

Tertullian, who is frequently called "the creator of ecclesiastical Latin," undoubtedly depended on earlier sources, including probably the "African Old Latin" version of the Scriptures. Nevertheless, it was from him, or certainly through him, that many words like "sacrament," and "trinity" passed into the theological vocabulary of Western Christendom. Schismatic and heretic though he was, he also is the fountainhead for much of the thought and the language of the mainstream of the church ever since.

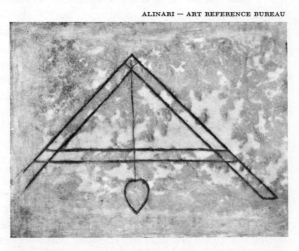

A drawing on a stone in the cemetery of Saint Callistus, dating from the second or third century. The triangular form symbolizes the Trinity. The plumb line, symbolizing uprightness, suggests the meaning and relevance of the Christian gospel.

Chapter Eleven

CLEMENT OF ALEXANDRIA

The Church and Intellectuals

ARE INTELLECT AND FAITH incompatible? Or are they mutually dependent upon one another? If mutually dependent, why does this not have more effect upon the lives of American churches? If incompatible, what distinctive characteristics of American Christianity make it so uncongenial to the life of thought and learning? Are there some problems of the intellectual in the church that can be blamed upon reactionary tendencies in the church? On the other hand, are there some problems of the intellectual in the church which are inherent in the ambiguities and qualities of the intellectual's own situation? Do intellectuals have something to learn from the church? Does the church have something to learn from the intellectuals? Should Christians encourage the development of a Christian *elite?*

Clement of Alexandria, the church father whom we consider in this chapter, lived at the opposite end of the Mediterranean from Tertullian's Carthage. The two men lived at about the same time, and the two cities were on the same continent. However, like the thousand miles of coastline separating the two cities, the worlds of Tertullian and Clement were widely separated both spiritually and intellectually.

Clement lived in the "university town" of Alexandria. A cosmopolitan, intellectual center of thought and learning, Alexandria was a natural location for showing how intellect and faith are mutually dependent upon one another. Clement was not primarily concerned to persuade persons outside the church about the reasonableness of the Christian claim. His major concern was to prove to Christian believers that Christ the Tutor could lead them to a fullness of knowledge and wisdom.

Before delving more deeply into the intellectual climate of third-century Alexandria, it would be helpful to construct a backdrop by visiting the first-century Corinthian congregation. The fact that the philosophers and intellectuals in the Mediterranean world of the first century had brought about deep hostility between the church and the intelligentsia is illustrated by a statement in Paul's first Letter to the Corinthians:

> Let no one deceive himself. If any one among you thinks that he is wise in this age, let him become a fool that he may become wise. For the wisdom of this world is folly with God. For it is written, "He catches the wise in their craftiness," and again, "The Lord knows that the thoughts of the wise are futile."
>
> *1 Corinthians 3:18–20*

Philo of Alexandria

As we have had occasion to note in chapter eight, the apologetic tradition associated with Justin and especially with Clement is actually older than Christianity itself, having many of its roots in the thought of the Jewish theologian Philo. This judgment is especially appropriate in the case of Clement, who not only is the first Christian writer to refer explicitly to Philo but who also borrows significantly from him. For one concept or metaphor after another in Clement, scholars have turned to Philo as a source and as an explanation.

Although it was once fashionable to think of Philo as a Jew who had incorporated into himself, consciously and unconsciously, the prevailing religious and intellectual character of his Gentile environment, a more careful study of his works and a comparison of their thought with rabbinic literature have led to a less superficial and more complex picture of Philo. He is now seen as a sophisticated but faithful adherent of the Jewish faith for whom neither simple assimilation nor traditional observance was sufficient. He is likewise a prototype, or example, of the Christian intellectuals of both East and West, who were to shape so much of the history of the theology of the church.

For our purposes in this chapter, two features of Philo's thought are of particular relevance. The first is his conviction that truth is ultimately one, and that therefore the message of biblical revelation and the philosophical search for the nature of things cannot permanently contradict each other. This conviction led him to treat philosophy sympathetically and to draw quite indiscriminately from various philosophical sources for his ideas about God, man, and the world.

Philo's thought led him, however, to a second conviction that was to be considered to be self-evident truth through most of Christian history—the principle that the deepest meaning of the Bible should be sought not in the simple historical sense of its words, phrases, and accounts, but in a figurative interpretation. Having begun with Greek efforts to make sense of Homer and Hesiod, this method of interpretation seemed to be applicable to Jewish scripture as well. In his minute commentaries on the accounts in the book of Genesis and on the life of Moses, Philo employed the allegorical method to harmonize his Greek philosophical ideas with his Jewish religious beliefs.

The Christian School at Alexandria

It is impossible to determine with any certainty just when Christianity first came to Alexandria. From the report about Apollos in Acts 18:24–28 it seems that some form of Christian teaching may have appeared among the Jews of Alexandria about the middle of the first century, although Apollos is said to have known "only the baptism of John." Perhaps the most noticeable gap in our knowledge of early church history is our almost complete lack of information about the history of Christianity in Alexandria and Egypt up to the year A.D. 180.

According to a tradition reported by Eusebius, the evangelist Mark is supposed to have founded churches in Alexandria and to have been succeeded as bishop of Alexandria by a man named Annianus. However, this report is difficult to verify. Nevertheless, various other references in Eusebius, Justin, Irenaeus, and Clement make it plausible that the beginnings of Alexandrian Christianity do date back to the first century. What is more, both Basilides and Valentinus, the Gnostic masters (see chapter seven), were active in Alexandria. This suggests the presence of a fairly advanced community of Christians interested in going beyond the simple faith of simple believers.

This ignorance about the beginnings of Alexandrian church history applies also to the origins of what is usually called "the catechetical school of Alexandria." Eusebius reports that about the

The Evangelist Mark and his symbol, the lion. According to a tradition reported by Eusebius, the evangelist Mark is supposed to have founded churches in Alexandria and to have been succeeded as bishop of Alexandria by a man named Annianus.

year 180 "there was a man of great renown for learning named Pantaenus, who had charge of the school of the faithful at Alexandria, where it has been a primitive custom that a school for sacred studies should exist. This school has continued even to our day."[1] Unfortunately, what Eusebius reports about Pantaenus is practically all that can be learned about him. It is also the earliest available information about the catechetical school. If we are to believe Eusebius and the unnamed sources on which he seems to depend, this school had begun even before Pantaenus, perhaps in the first half of the second century. Some recent scholars have questioned the existence of such a catechetical school before the time of Clement or even before that of Origen, and it is certainly a mistake to think of it in the formal sense usually indicated to us by the word "school"; but such extreme skepticism has perhaps gone too far.

The early appearance of Gnostic teachers in Alexandria, to which we have already referred, may also help to explain the beginnings of the catechetical school as a place where the dialogue between Christianity and Greek philosophy was carried on under Christian auspices. Later on, under Clement and Origen, the school gave instruction not only in the Bible and in Christian theology, but in secular and classical learning as well. It seems that the revulsion of Socrates and Plato at the mercenary nature of the Sophist teachers * of their day was shared by the Christians of the catechetical school, for its students were not required to pay tuition fees. They were, however, permitted to make voluntary contributions. In addition, the school sought support for its teachers from patrons. All of this would fit in well with Clement's own characterization of Pantaenus, his teacher, as one who "gathering the spoil of the flowers of the prophetic and apostolic meadow, engendered in the souls of his hearers a deathless element of knowledge,"[2] and with the report of Eusebius that Pantaenus, like Justin, had come to the Christian faith after an earlier involvement with Greek philosophy.

At the center of the curriculum of the catechetical school, however, was the Bible; and instruction was devoted principally to its interpretation. Like its pagan and secular counterparts, the school

---

* Sophists were teachers in ancient Greece who became prominent during the fifth century B.C. They were the first teachers to offer anything approaching systematic "higher" education, and they were paid for instruction. Their opinions were often considered to be unorthodox.

The earliest-known representation of catechetical instruction, dating from the second century. The teacher expounds the Scriptures to two men. The water clock on the left was common in schoolrooms.

trained its students to employ grammar, philology, and textual study as means of penetrating to a fuller grasp of a sacred book. This, in turn, would resolve the apparent contradictions between revelation and reason. Nowhere in the ancient world, not even in Rome, was there a more brilliant setting for Christian speculation and scholarship than Alexandria.

"A Man Virtuous and Approved"

Into this heady intellectual atmosphere came Clement, or, to use his full name, Titus Flavius Clemens. He seems to have been born in Athens about A.D. 150, of pagan parents. Eusebius speaks of Clement as having come from paganism to Christianity, but we cannot gather anything specific about Clement's conversion either from his own writings or from any reliable tradition. His studies were occupied both with Christian subjects and with the pagan writers, with whom he shows a familiarity that encompasses poets as well as philosophers. After visiting other centers he was drawn to Alexandria, and particularly to Pantaenus, under whom he studied. He also appears to have been ordained a presbyter in the church of Alexandria.

About A.D. 190 he began to offer instruction in the catechetical school, eventually succeeding his teacher Pantaenus. From the report that in A.D. 202 "there was no one at Alexandria set apart for catechetical instruction, for all had been driven away by the threat of the persecution,"[3] it is usually concluded that Clement was driven out by the persecution under Septimius Severus, who was emperor from A.D. 193 to 211.

The next report that we have of Clement, and the final one, comes from a letter written by Bishop Alexander in A.D. 211 and preserved by Eusebius.

> This letter I send unto you, my dear brethren, by the hand of Clement the blessed presbyter, a man virtuous and approved, of whom ye yourselves also have heard, and with whom ye will become acquainted; who, when he was present here in the providence and oversight of the Master, both stablished and increased the church of the Lord.[4]

Another letter by Alexander, dated 216, speaks of Clement as dead. Thus he must have died between A.D. 211 and 216.

Clement was a prolific writer with far-ranging interests, but of the many books he is credited with having written, only four have come down to us. Surely the most readable is a little treatise entitled *Who Is the Rich Man That Shall Be Saved?* a commentary on the story in Mark 10:17–31. There is such a close connection between the other three works, or at least between the first two of them, that they are often called a trilogy. The *Protrepticus,* like other works of the same title written by Aristotle, Epicurus, Cleanthes, and others, is a hortatory discourse. Its theme is the superiority of Christianity to the doctrines of paganism. In *The Tutor,* Clement describes Christ the Logos as the heavenly Teacher of the soul, who guides it through the changes and chances of this present life.

There is no similar unifying theme in the *Stromateis,* a title that refers literally to bags in which such things as bedclothes were kept. Thus we would perhaps call the book *Grab Bags* or, more formally, *Miscellanies.* Here Clement speaks of many of the topics treated in the other two books and contrasts the authentic Christian gnosis with both the moral practices and the theological teachings of the heretical Gnostics. Fragments of one or two other writings survive, but these four writings are the only complete works still available.

The First Christian Scholar

Clement has been called the first Christian scholar. Like most of his contemporaries—and like most scholars since—he obtained some of his learning from studying handbooks and collections of quotations rather than from studying all the classics personally; but this should not disqualify him. He was learned enough to arouse the suspicions of many heresy-hunters in subsequent ages! In fact, Pope Clement VIII had Clement's name removed from the catalog of the saints because of such suspicions. In many ways his thought and career epitomize the dilemma of the intellectual in the church, who seeks to be a loyal citizen of two realms that have often declared constant war upon each other. Although later Greek fathers such as Origen and Gregory of Nyssa struggled with many of the same problems, Clement's predicament is both the earliest and in some ways the most touching in the long history of that war.

A fundamental element in this predicament is Clement's idea of a Christian *elite*. Christ "did not certainly disclose to the many what did not belong to the many; but to the few to whom he knew that they belonged, who were capable of receiving and being moulded according to them." [5] Naturally Clement knew himself to be part of this "elite" and thus to have a share in this secret tradition.

The analogies between Clement's notion of an élite and the heretical Gnostic classification of men into the material, the psychic, and the spiritual are more than coincidental. Still there is this fundamental difference: Clement speaks as an intellectual *in the church*, obedient to its revealed faith and responsible to its fellowship, while the Gnostics regarded all of this as beneath their dignity. The legitimacy of the label "an intellectual" for Clement is evident from the central role of the intellect and reason in his theology and personal piety.

The dominant recurring theme of Clement's thought is the conception of Christ as the Logos, the Word of God. One of his favorite biblical passages, cited over and over in his writings, is John 1:3: "All things were made through him [the Logos], and without him was not anything made that was made." In his discussion of the doctrine of creation, therefore, Clement concentrates on the role of the preexistent Logos in the formation of the world and especially in the constitution of the human race. The Logos is the principle of structure in the universe and of reason in man. Now, however, the Logos had come to earth as the Tutor of men, and his instruction had enabled them to attain salvation.

Clement's theological system is uneven and incomplete. As we shall see in chapter twelve, Origen developed many of Clement's suggestions into full-blown speculations. Nevertheless, the importance of Clement for the history of Christian speculation is enormous. Harnack says:

> His great work, which has rightly been called the boldest literary undertaking in the history of the church, is . . . the first attempt to use holy Scriptures and the church tradition together with the asssumption that Christ as the Reason of the world is the source of all truth, as the basis of a presentation of Christianity which at once addresses itself to the cultured by satisfying the scientific demand for a philosophical ethic and theory of the world, and at the same time reveals to the believer the rich content of his faith.[6]

Almost every examination of the place of the intellectual in the church and of the relation between Christ and culture finds itself obliged to consider Clement's view of the Logos as the Christ of culture and also the Christ above all culture.

Clement of Alexandria succeeded better than the apologists discussed in chapter eight in his attempt to show other Christians that the life of reason and the life of faith, far from being incompatible, are in fact dependent on each other.

Chapter Twelve
ORIGEN OF ALEXANDRIA

The Interpretation of Scripture

SHOULD WE INTERPRET scripture literally or as allegory? (Allegory involves the expression of truth by means of symbolic figures and actions. Persons and events are figurative and symbolic.)

Christians have been—and are—on both sides of this fence, for the issue is a complex one. If, for example, all of the Scriptures are interpreted literally, how is the thought and life of the church to make Christian sense of vast stretches of Old Testament narrative? On the other hand, if one turns to allegorical, or symbolic, interpretation, does this not open the way to the abuses of private and individual interpretation—without control or discipline? Luther said that allegory made the Bible into a nose of wax that anyone could twist as he chose.

As we shall see in more detail later in this chapter, Origen claimed value for an allegorical interpretation of parts of the Bible; he felt that in this way the Old Testament stands with equality alongside of the New Testament. Origen could point to allegorical interpretation by the apostle Paul himself. Even the word "allegory" itself appears in Paul's interpretations, in Galatians 4:24: "Now this is an allegory." In Galatians 4:21–31, Paul takes part of the Old Testament narrative about the patriarchs and interprets it as an allegory of the two covenants—of the law and of the gospel. Neither here nor elsewhere does Paul indicate the legitimacy or the limits of such interpretation, but this is by no means an isolated instance in his use of Hebrew scripture.

In the Old Testament, the Song of Solomon is interesting to examine in the light of the question of how to interpret the Scriptures. In its actual origin, the Song of Solomon may well have been a love poem of the erotic sort quite familiar in the literature of the ancient Near East. By the time it was finally accepted into the Christian canon of Holy Scripture, however, it was being read as an allegory of the relation between God and his people, or between Christ and the church. Ever since, the Song of Solomon has been interpreted allegorically rather than literally. How else could such sensual verse remain within the Christian Bible?

A Cradle Christian

Unlike most of the church fathers with whom we have been dealing, Origen was born a Christian. The date of his birth is about A.D. 186. The place is Egypt, probably Alexandria.

As often happens to great men, Origen's childhood and youth later became the subject of many legends. As Eusebius says in his account of the life of Origen, which occupies a large part of Book VI of his *Ecclesiastical History*, "I think that even the facts from his very cradle, so to speak, are worthy of mention." [1]

Even when one makes allowance for the legendary flavor of some of these accounts, however, it is obvious that Origen developed outstanding qualities much earlier in life than is normally the case. His father, Leonidas, recognized his unusual endowments.

> He rejoiced greatly and thanked God, the author of all good, that he had deemed him worthy to be the father of such a child. And they say that often, standing by the boy when asleep, he uncovered his breast as if the divine Spirit were enshrined within it, and kissed it reverently; considering himself blessed in his goodly offspring. [2]

Leonidas was martyred when Origen was seventeen years old. The training in the Bible and in Greek literature that Origen had received from his father was then supplemented by study under others, including (according to Eusebius) Clement of Alexandria. Shortly after his father's death Origen was entrusted with responsibility for teaching in the catechetical school (see chapter eleven) and soon was in charge. As a teacher, he attracted hearers from all around, not only Christian catechumens but heretics and even pagan philosophers. He also studied philosophy with the influential Neoplatonic philosopher, Ammonius Saccas.* Origen's study of philoso-

---

* Neoplatonism, or New Platonism, originated in the city of Alexandria about A.D. 200. It modified the teachings of Plato to accord with Aristotelian and Oriental conceptions.

phy was only a means to an end, however. That end was the service of the church through the exposition, or interpretation, of the Scriptures. When the number of students in his classes became too large for him to handle, he entrusted the elementary pupils to an associate and concentrated on the instruction of those who could grasp an advanced exposition of the Bible.

So widespread was the fame of Origen that at various times both the pagan governor of Egypt and Julia Mamaea, the mother of the Emperor Alexander Severus, summoned him to them for an interview. He also traveled elsewhere—to Rome, to Arabia, to Caesarea in Palestine. On one of Origen's visits to Caesarea—the records are quite confusing on this question as on many others in the life of Origen—he was ordained a presbyter, an action that aroused the anger of his bishop in Alexandria, who recalled him to Alexandria, deposed him from the priesthood and from his teaching position, and forced him to go into exile. This happened in A.D. 231 and 232. From Alexandria, Origen went to Caesarea, this time to stay, although he did visit Athens and Arabia after settling in Caesarea.

Origen died at the age of sixty-nine in the city of Tyre, and according to Jerome was buried there. His grave was a tourist attraction as late as the thirteenth century. From boyhood he had cherished a desire for martyrdom and had been restrained from it then only by a trick of his mother, who hid his clothes. Yet he did not die a martyr, although he underwent great sufferings shortly before his death, in the persecution of the church under Emperor Decius.

The Interpreter of the Holy Spirit

Above all, Origen was a student of the Bible. The sheer amount of his biblical study and learning is overwhelming. Hans Lietzmann has said that "Origen lived in the Bible to an extent which perhaps no one else has rivalled, except Luther." [3] As part of his task of biblical scholarship, Origen prepared an immense edition of the Old Testament in six columns (hence its title, *Hexapla*): the Hebrew text, a Greek transliteration of the Hebrew text, the Greek translation of Aquila (about A.D. 140), the Greek translation of Symmachus (from the second half of the second century A.D.), the Septuagint translation of the Old Testament into Greek (from the third and the second century A.D.), and Theodotion's revision of the Septuagint (from the second century A.D.). In addition some portions of the work contained as many as three additional Greek versions. From the testimony of Jerome almost two centuries later it is clear that the *Hexapla*, in fifty volumes, was preserved in Origen's library at Caesarea; and from medieval usage it is evident that portions of it were copied, translated, and circulated long afterwards.

The *Hexapla* was merely a preparation for the assignment that Origen set himself of expounding almost every book of both the Old and the New Testament, either in commentaries or in sermons or in both. We are fortunate in possessing a contemporary account of the effect that these expositions had on their hearers. One of Origen's pupils, a man named Gregory whom Origen converted to Christianity, wrote an extravagant and moving tribute to his teacher, in which he declared: "Of all men now living, I have never known or heard of one who had pondered as he had on the pure and luminous words [of the Scriptures] and had become so expert at fathoming their meaning and teaching them to others. The Spirit who inspires the prophets and all divine and mystic discourse honored him as a friend and appointed him his interpreter." [4]

Origen's work as "the interpreter of the Holy Spirit" was subsidized for many years by Ambrose, a rich man who had formerly been an adherent of Valentinian Gnosticism. With the help of Ambrose, Origen managed to keep seven stenographers and seven transcribers busy. Late in life he was persuaded to permit his lectures and sermons to be taken down also, thus increasing his literary output tremendously.

As a biblical interpreter, Origen is remembered for his adherence to the allegorical method. He was convinced that "the Holy Spirit willed that the figures of the mysteries [of the faith] should be roofed over in the divine Scriptures, and should not be displayed publicly, and in the open air." [5] Therefore the Scriptures were not being interpreted adequately when the expositor remained content with the literal, historical sense of the words. He needed to penetrate to the spiritual, invisible sense, "to the intent that we may utter not the things that the ear of the flesh perceives, but those that are contained within the Spirit's will." [6]

These statements come from Origen's commentary on the Song of Solomon which, whatever its origins, had been interpreted as an allegory by the rabbis and was later to become the book most read and most often commented upon in the medieval cloister. Did like principles of interpretation apply to books of the Bible that seem to be obviously intended as histories, such as the Book of Joshua? Origen's *Homilies on Joshua* take the phrase "to this day" (Joshua 15:63) as proof that the text is not to be understood literally.

> Taking our beginning from the literal sense, we want to ask those who think that this text can be understood literally, what does it mean when it says, 'to this day'? . . . Let us, however, understand this according to the spiritual sense.[7]

The story of Jonah from an early Christian stone relief on a sarcophagus (limestone coffin). This was one of the earliest and most prevalent themes of catacomb art—involving the allegorical method in depicting redemption and salvation.

Modern scholars are not agreed about whether Origen ever maintained that only the allegorical sense was the right one or whether he sought to base the allegorical sense on the literal sense; but he certainly believed that the literal sense was inadequate, and at least in that sense erroneous, by itself. They are agreed about his importance. One scholar writes:

> It was due to Origen, more than to any other single master, that one of the most extensive branches of Christian literature, that of biblical interpretation, and one of the principal divisions of Christian thought, that of biblical theology, were established for all time in the center of the activity of the church.[8]

Curiously, Origen's activity as "the interpreter of the Holy Spirit" and of the Holy Scriptures did not figure prominently in the usual summaries of his thought by church historians, being overshadowed by the speculative and controversial issues of his theology. One of the most significant contributions of present-day scholarship is the restoration of Origen's work as an interpreter of the Bible to its central place in his career.

The First System of Doctrine

Biblical interpreter though he was, Origen was also the author of what has been understood as the first attempt to supply a complete system of Christian doctrine, the book entitled *On First Principles.* He also continued and brought to fruition the work of the Apologists (see chapter eight) in his treatise *Against Celsus,* which has been called by its modern editor, Professor Henry Chadwick, "the culmination of the whole apologetic movement of the second and third centuries."[9] These works were the only ones deemed worthy of inclusion in the standard English edition of the church fathers published in the nineteenth century. They are likewise the works in which Origen expressed most of the speculative and systematic teachings for which he was condemned by later centuries.

Because of Origen's importance for the history of the relation between speculation and faith, we turn now to these two works, particularly to the former, and to the controversial opinions expressed there in opposition to what was to become the orthodox teaching of the church.

It is important to note that we are speaking of what was to become orthodox after Origen, not of what was orthodox already. He was determined to teach only what had been approved by the church on those issues where the church had spoken. "I desire," he said of himself, "to be a man of the church and to be named and designated not from the title of some heresiarch [originator or supporter of a heresy], but from that of Christ; in my work as well as in my thought I want to be a Christian and to be called one." [10] When he came to discuss doctrine, therefore, he sought to specify what he had called the teaching of the church and to distinguish in it what had not been explained with enough clarity. About this latter he felt both permitted and obliged to speculate: permitted because the church had not formulated its doctrine, obliged because the definition and the defense of Christianity would not be complete without an airing of these very issues.

As Origen proceeded with his speculations, he naturally drew upon the best available thought, both Christian and pagan, just as he drew upon Jewish and pagan as well as upon Christian principles of interpretation in his explanations of the Bible. It was particularly from the followers of Plato, from what we now call "Middle Platonism," that he derived many of his ideas. In mixture with the teachings of the church, these ideas are accused of having produced—for example, in the area of eschatology, the doctrine of the end of the world and the second coming of Christ—what Hanson has called "not a Platonized form of genuine Christian eschatology, but an alternative to eschatology, indeed an evasion of it." [11]

There are three doctrinal issues about which Origen speculated in a way that was to earn him the condemnation of the orthodox. The most crucial of these issues was his attempt to make sense of the church's language about Jesus Christ. A century after the death of Origen, the church was engaged in a deep and bitter struggle about this language. We shall give some consideration to that struggle in chapter sixteen. Interestingly, both sides in the struggle cited the authority of Origen—and both of them were partly right! On the one hand, Origen taught that the Logos (Word) had been generated and begotten eternally. On the other hand, he taught also that the Logos was subordinate to the Father. Origen spoke in one way as a biblical theologian, in another way as a speculative philosopher, and in yet another way as an apologist against the accusations of Celsus. Also, he was attempting to articulate the faith of the church in opposition to the notion that Father, Son, and Holy Spirit are merely three modes of divine revelation. It was to Origen that the church owed the insistence, which was to be basic to orthodox theology ever after, that each of the three is a distinct person. To guarantee that distinctness, however, Origen felt obliged to subordinate the Son to the Father. This conflicted with the later doctrine of Christian orthodoxy, even though it also made this doctrine possible.

A second issue, which Origen related to the first, was the pre-existence of souls. In common with the "Middle Platonists" to whom he bears such a close resemblance in some ways, Origen seems to have taught that the souls which now inhabit human bodies existed before those bodies were created, and that they fell from the holiness and simplicity for which they were made into a lower form of existence; namely, individuality. This finally equates creation and the fall, and for that reason the theory was condemned. Nevertheless, it was intended as a way of accounting for man's fallen state (eventually explained by Augustine's doctrine of original sin).

The third speculative doctrine for which Origen became notorious dealt with the end of history rather than with its beginning. Taking his cue from the biblical phrase, "the restitution of all things" (Acts 3:21, *King James Version*), Origen—for once—interpreted the word "all" literally, and taught that not only man and other parts of the cosmic creation, but the fallen angels and Satan himself would be restored. Even death and Satan would yield to the completeness of the restoration.

All three of these speculative doctrines came under orthodox fire in later centuries, and deservedly so. Each of them, consistently carried out, would have threatened basic Christian affirmations about God and his work of creation and redemption. However, it was largely because Origen had raised these questions that the church councils of later centuries included them in their agenda. What is more, the solutions set forth for these questions by the councils and by the orthodox fathers were based upon the analysis, the vocabulary, and the conceptual framework furnished by the works of Origen. One of the most impeccably orthodox of those fathers, the celebrated Gregory of Nyssa (died around A.D. 395), was able to take over even Origen's doctrine of the restoration of all things and to work it into a system of speculative thought that conformed with the dogmatic faith of the church.

The crucial significance of Origen for the history of Christian thought, therefore, is almost beyond exaggeration. The church is indebted to Origen for the fact that Christianity is a rational faith. The entire educated world is in his debt for the preservation of the old Hellenic intellectual culture, which he transformed into the beginnings of a system of doctrine for Christianity. We may perhaps be permitted to add that, in spite of their adverse criticism concerning him, neither Martin Luther nor John Calvin could have been the theologian he was if he had not drawn, indirectly and unconsciously, on a tradition of which Origen of Alexandria was one of the chief sources of thought.

The marble statue of Hippolytus, dating from about A.D. *238. This is the earliest-known Christian portrait statue. Hippolytus, theologian and bishop of Rome, made a calculation of the date for Easter for many years ahead. These dates are inscribed on the throne of the statuary, and are visible in this picture. Also inscribed on the throne is a list of his writings.*

Chapter Thirteen
HIPPOLYTUS

Is There a Role for Ritual?

No CHURCH CAN UNDERTAKE the formulation or the practice of rituals without thinking of the meanings that underlie them or that can be derived from them. The liturgical tradition of the United Church of Christ, bringing together the usages of Puritanism and those of Continental Protestantism, is a good case study both of the inevitability of ritual and of the problems involved in any liturgical reform. How *does* a church go about developing a ritual for worship?

In the present chapter we "visit" with Hippolytus, and turn to a study of the ritual of Christian worship. It should become clear that in many respects the liturgy of Hippolytus bears the marks of its historical origins. Both its ecclesiastical and its cultural settings are reflected in its forms and language. In another cultural and ecclesiastical setting, therefore, many of these forms simply would not fit. On the other hand, many of the forms that might be suggested as replacements for them would not commend themselves as any more appropriate.

The question now arises almost spontaneously: What, if any, is the role of ritual in Christian worship?

A Schismatic and a Saint

The most detailed evidence we have about the rituals of at least one section of the early church comes down to us in a brief treatise entitled *The Apostolic Tradition*. In the almost unanimous judgment of modern scholars, this document was written by Hippolytus of Rome. The history of his career is extremely hard to piece together. Eusebius, who was born only about a fourth of a century after the death of Hippolytus, knew so little about him that all he could say was: "And likewise also Hippolytus, who also presided over another church somewhere." [1] Eusebius did know at least the titles of several books by Hippolytus. Even Jerome, who was better informed about the Western church than Eusebius had been, was obliged to confess: "I have not been able to discover the name of his city." [2]

A most remarkable source of information about the writings of Hippolytus is a statue unearthed in Rome in 1551, portraying a churchman seated on a chair. The titles of many of the works of Hippolytus are inscribed on the statue. From various indications, archaeologists and historians have concluded that the statue was probably executed during the lifetime of Hippolytus. Additional data about his life have come from the discovery of his book, *Refutation of All Heresies,* from which some of the facts about Gnosticism reported in chapter six were derived.

On the basis of these and other materials it is possible to reconstruct at least part of Hippolytus' story. Neither the place nor the date of his birth is known. From his use of the Greek language, from his acquaintance with Greek literature, and from some of the emphases of his theology, however, it has been surmised that he came from Alexandria or from Asia Minor.

We first meet Hippolytus in Rome, where Origen heard him lecture, presumably in A.D. 212. This suggests that Hippolytus was in good standing at that time; but shortly thereafter he accused the bishop of Rome, Zephyrinus, of heresy in the doctrine of Christ. Zephyrinus died in A.D. 217 and was succeeded by Callistus, against whom Hippolytus raged even more vehemently, attacking him both for his theology and for his lax administration of church discipline— his willingness to admit those guilty of adultery and fornication to communion. His opposition to Callistus led Hippolytus to separate from the church at Rome and to lead a schismatic party, of which he became bishop.

The schism seems to have continued for almost two decades, during which Urban and Pontian served as the successors of Callistus. A third-century catalog of the bishops of Rome reports: "At that time Pontian the bishop and Hippolytus the presbyter were banished and deported to the unhealthy island of Sardinia in the consulship of Severus and Quintian"; that is, in A.D. 235. [3] From the language of this catalog it appears that Hippolytus died on Sardinia, and that he was being honored in Rome within two decades of his death. Present-day scholars are inclined to believe that Pontian and Hippolytus were reconciled in exile, if not even earlier.

By the latter part of the fourth century Hippolytus was highly regarded in Rome as a martyr. He is still a saint in both the Eastern and the Western churches.

The Eucharistic Ritual

Although Hippolytus is notable for several writings, our interest here is concentrated on *The Apostolic Tradition,* which has been laboriously reconstructed from various translations. It describes the liturgies and prayers that were used for the ordination of several ranks of clergy and for the observance of various ordinances. It also contains rules about Christian conduct. Two sections of the treatise supply information about the ritual of the celebration of the Lord's Supper. The first is the text of the "eucharistic prayer," or prayer of

GIRAUDON

A sixth- or seventh-century silver paten, depicting the communion of the apostles. Christ is shown giving bread and wine.

thanksgiving and of consecration. The second is an account of the liturgical actions of the celebration. The two sections seem important enough to be reproduced here, for any summary would be inadequate and would probably be lengthier than the texts.

> To him [the bishop] then let the deacons bring the oblation [eucharistic elements to be offered in worship] and he with all the presbyters laying his hand on the oblation shall say giving thanks: "The Lord be with you." And the people shall say: "And with thy spirit." And the bishop shall say: "Lift up your hearts." And the people shall say: "We have them with the Lord." And the bishop shall say: "Let us give thanks unto the Lord." And the people shall say: "It is meet and right." And forthwith he shall continue thus: "We render thanks unto thee, O God, through thy beloved Child Jesus Christ, whom in the last times thou didst send to us to be a Savior and Redeemer and the Messenger of thy counsel; who is thy Word inseparable from thee, through whom thou madest all things and in whom thou wast well-pleased; whom thou didst send from heaven into the Virgin's womb and who, conceived within her, was made flesh and demonstrated to by thy Son, being born of Holy Spirit and a Virgin; who fulfilling thy will and preparing for thee a holy people, stretched forth his hands for suffering, that he might release from sufferings them who have believed in thee; who when he was betrayed to voluntary suffering that he might abolish death and rend the bonds of the devil and tread down hell and enlighten the righteous and establish the ordinance and demonstrate the resurrection: taking bread and giving thanks to thee, said: "Take, eat: this is my body which is broken for you." Likewise also the cup, saying: "This is my blood, which is shed for you. When ye do this ye do my remembrance." Doing therefore the remembrance of his death and resurrection, we offer to thee the bread and the cup, making eucharist to thee because thou hast bidden us to stand before thee and minister as priests to thee. And we pray thee that thou wouldest grant to all thy saints who partake to be united that they may be fulfilled with the Holy Spirit for the confirmation of their faith in truth, that we may praise and glorify thee through thy Child Jesus Christ, through whom glory and honor be unto thee with the Holy Spirit in thy holy church now and forever and world without end. Amen.[4]

Christians who find portions of this foregoing prayer familiar because of its similarities with the "epiclesis" (liturgical invocation of the Holy Spirit for the purpose of consecrating the eucharistic elements) of the Divine Liturgy of Eastern Orthodoxy or with the "eucharistic prayers" of some Anglican and Lutheran rites would nevertheless feel strange if they witnessed a celebration of the sacrament based on the following order:

41369

Then let the oblation at once be brought by the deacons to the bishop, and he shall eucharistize first the bread into the representation of the flesh of Christ; and the cup mixed with wine for the antitype [that which corresponds] of the blood which was shed for all who have believed in him; and milk and honey mingled together in fulfillment of the promise which was made to the fathers, wherein he said, "I will give you a land flowing with milk and honey"; which Christ indeed gave, even his flesh, whereby they who believe are nourished like little children, making the bitterness of the human heart sweet by the sweetness of his word; water also for an oblation for a sign of the laver [baptism], that the inner man also, which is psychic, may receive the same rites as the body. And the bishop shall give an explanation concerning all these things to them who receive. And when he breaks the bread in distributing to each a fragment he shall say: "The bread of heaven in Christ Jesus." And he who receives shall answer: "Amen." And the presbyters—but if there are not enough of them the deacons also—shall hold the cups and stand by in good order and with reverence: first he that holdeth the water, second he who holds the milk, third he who holds the wine. And they who partake shall taste of each cup thrice, he who gives it saying: "In God the Father Almighty"; and he who receives shall say: "Amen." "And in the Lord Jesus Christ"; and he shall say: "Amen." "And in the Holy Spirit and in the Holy Church"; and he shall say: "Amen." So shall it be done to each one.[5]

A rubbing of a wooden seal used to imprint the Greek eucharistic bread called "prosphora." Prosphora means "to carry" (early Christians brought bread and wine to the church for use during services), and refers to a leavened bread, round and in two layers, signifying the two natures of Christ.

Chapter Fourteen
CYPRIAN OF CARTHAGE

The Politics of Polity

The Apostolic Tradition of Hippolytus reflects customs of the Roman church at the beginning of the third century. It represents also the effort of the church in the third century to find apostolic sanction for its liturgical customs.

Still more important, as we have seen already in chapter two, was the apostolic validity of the organizational structure of the church. The task of clarifying what this implied was shared by many church leaders of the second and third centuries. However, none of them shaped its eventual solution more decisively than Cyprian of Carthage. The solution that Cyprian was so instrumental in forging was what has come to be called an episcopal polity—the government of the church by bishops or by a hierarchy such as bishops, elders, and deacons.

Cyprian doubtless knew that Paul had written: "This is why I [Paul] left you [Titus] in Crete, that you might amend what was defective, and appoint elders in every town as I directed you" (Titus 1:5). Yet difficult questions remained: Did Paul mean that his authority as an apostle was transferable to someone like Titus, and transferable in turn from Titus to subsequent bishops? If so, what guarantees were there for the legitimacy of the process? If not, what was to be the form of apostolic authenticity and authority?

It is interesting to note that these are the selfsame questions currently receiving intensive and extensive study by representatives of the six churches in the Consultation on Church Union:

> Varying degrees of importance are affixed to apostolic succession, or (more accurately) the historic episcopate. Is continuity with the

apostolic faith guaranteed by an historical succession of ecclesiastical officials, or does apostolicity hinge on the ministry's persistence in mission and faithfulness to the apostolic gospel? Is the historic episcopate mandatory for a valid ministry in the church? [1]

In a report on "One Ministry" adopted at the Princeton meeting in April, 1964, the churches in the Consultation on Church Union made the following affirmation.

We believe that in a servant church that is truly catholic, truly reformed, and truly evangelical, the ministerial orders should include the historic ministries of bishops, presbyters (elders), and deacons although we acknowledge that the particular functions of these ministries require further clarification. [2]

The process of "further clarification" thrusts conferees into the heart of what has long been regarded as the Achilles' heel of the ecumenical movement. In this thorny but significant process, helpful perspective and invaluable insight can be gathered from the trip back into history—especially from a visit with Cyprian of Carthage.

Bishop of Carthage

Cyprian was the subject of what has been called "the first Christian biography," attributed to his deacon, Pontius. However, his own writings, especially his letters, are historically more reliable. He was born a pagan, of a wealthy family, in the first decade of the third century. He was trained as an orator, and not until he was an adult did he come to the Christian faith. Soon thereafter he was ordained a presbyter. In A.D. 248 or 249 he was elected bishop of Carthage.

The persecution of the church under the Emperor Decius in A.D. 250 forced Cyprian to flee, as he said, "taking into consideration not so much my own safety as the public peace of the brethren . . . lest, by my overbold presence, the tumult which had begun might be still further provoked." [3] During his absence the church at Carthage became embroiled in a controversy about the proper treatment of "the lapsed"—those who had, in one way or another, compromised their faith during the persecution. Upon his return in A.D. 251, Cyprian upheld the position that the lapsed should be permitted to do public penance and to return to the fellowship of the church—although this latter might in some cases be delayed until the hour of their death. A new persecution broke out in A.D. 257 and Cyprian was banished. On September 14, 258, he was beheaded, "the first one who in Africa imbued his priestly crown with the blood of martyrdom." [4]

Cyprian's best-known works are his treatises *The Lapsed* and *The Unity of the Catholic Church,* both of which are concerned with the nature of the church as one, holy, catholic, and apostolic. It will not do violence to Cyprian's thought if we summarize the contents of those treatises under these four concepts.

The church is one. "This holy mystery of oneness, this unbreakable bond of close-knit harmony is portrayed in the gospel by our Lord Jesus Christ's coat, which was not divided or cut at all, but when they drew lots for the vesture of Christ to see which of them should put on Christ, it was the whole coat that was won, the garment was acquired unspoiled and undivided." [5]

The church is holy. The lapsed must perform acts of penitence before being readmitted to the fellowship of the church, for "no one is in union with the church who cuts himself off from the gospel." [6]

The church is catholic. "He who is not in the church of Christ is not a Christian," for he is acting "in spite of God's tradition, in spite of the combined and everywhere compacted unity of the Catholic church." [7]

BY THE COURTESY OF THE TUNISIAN EMBASSY, LONDON.

Large mosaic baptismal font dedicated to the "Most blessed Saint Cyprian." The font, which dates from the sixth century, was excavated in 1952 near Carthage.

The church is apostolic. For, in a statement that has been in controversy between Roman Catholics and Protestants, "it is on one man [Peter] that he [Christ] builds the church, and although he assigns a like power to all the apostles after his resurrection, . . . yet, in order that the oneness might be unmistakable, he established by his own authority a source for that oneness." [8]

The Church Is in the Bishop

According to Cyprian, the church does not have these concepts in abstract principle, but in the concrete structures of its organizational life. Specifically, it is the church's clergy, and in particular the bishops, who represent and guarantee the unity, the holiness, the catholicity, and the apostolicity of the church. For "the bishop is in the church, and the church is in the bishop. . . . The church, which is catholic and one, is not cut nor divided, but is indeed connected and bound together by the cement of priests who cohere with one another." [9]

So convinced was Cyprian of the decisive place of the bishop in the life of the church that his views on this question became a central issue in the theological controversies of the following century. One of Cyprian's solutions for the problem of dealing with the lapsed was to argue that the holiness of the church does not depend on the holiness of its individual members, but that the validity of its sacraments does depend on the bishops' innocence of mortal sin. "In this he was both maintaining the former tradition of the [North African] church as represented by Tertullian, and preparing the ground for the Donatists," [10] who taught that the moral compromise of certain Catholic bishops, specifically their performance of acts of pagan sacrifice under the threat of Roman persecution, had brought about the fall of the church.

In opposition to the Donatists, Augustine was to argue that the validity of the sacraments did not depend on the personal holiness of the one administering them, but on the objective ordinance of Christ. The bitterness of the controversy with the Donatists is evidence for the tenacity of the doctrine championed by Cyprian.

A related issue is Cyprian's relation to the see of Rome. The words quoted earlier about the centrality of Peter among the apostles have, as we indicated, been a subject of much controversy—as has, of course, the saying of Jesus in Matthew 16:18 on which they form a

105

commentary. To make matters worse, there exist in the manuscript tradition two versions of these words from Cyprian's *The Unity of the Catholic Church*. One version seems to say that it is Peter as part of the apostolic body who is authoritative; the other seems to stress the uniqueness of Peter more specifically. At one time Protestants thought of the latter of these as a Roman forgery, and some Roman Catholics claimed that the first was an anti-Roman forgery. Most scholars today would probably agree with the conclusion of the massive research of the Roman Catholic scholar, Maurice Bévenot, who has maintained that both versions come from Cyprian himself. He believes that the "papal" version is the earlier one, and that Cyprian rewrote it when it was being interpreted in a manner contrary to his original intention, in a way that asserted the primacy of the see of Rome.

The problem of the fourth chapter of Cyprian's *The Unity of the Catholic Church* is rendered even more interesting by his concrete relations with Rome. The bishop of Rome, Stephen I, who died in A.D. 257, taught, in opposition to the rigorists, that a baptism performed by a heretic could be valid if it met the requirements of the ordinance of Christ. Cyprian, on the other hand, contended vigorously for the position, as he expressed it in a letter to Stephen, "that those who have been dipped abroad outside the church, and have been stained among heretics and schismatics with the taint of profane water, when they come to us and to *the church which is one,* ought to be baptized. . . . That is not baptism which the heretics use." [11]

Despite the vehemence of Cyprian's attacks on Stephen, the unity of the church (referred to in the words we have italicized in the preceding quotation) remained uppermost in his mind. And it was in the name of Cyprian's dedication to unity that in the century which followed Augustine refuted the Donatist doctrine that the impurity of a bishop obligated Christians to separate themselves from him and from all of those who had been baptized by him. Ironically, then, Cyprian attacked the bishop of Rome in stronger language than any of the other fathers of the early church. Yet by his insistence on the unity of the church and by his emphasis on the centrality of the bishop he made a substantial contribution to the eventual development of the Roman papacy and of the form of church government known as episcopal.

Chapter Fifteen

EUSEBIUS

The Christianization of the Empire

THE FATHERS OF THE EARLY CHURCH whom we have been studying in this book all belong to the group designated "Ante-Nicene Fathers"—those whose careers precede A.D. 325, the year of the epochmaking Council of Nicaea. We have made this date the terminus of our narrative in order to be able to encompass a manageable body of material. The changes in the life of the church achieved under the Emperor Constantine and symbolized by the Council of Nicaea were so drastic and so profound that 325 is one of the most decisive lines of demarcation in Western history—far more decisive than most of the arbitrary divisions of history into "eras" in the conventional textbooks. There was a drastic change from hostility—including open persecution—to governmental sanction and support.

Nevertheless, in two final chapters we are going beyond our selfimposed limit to describe the lives and careers of two men who were present at the Council of Nicaea but who continued to be active after the council. The inclusion of these two men, Eusebius and Athanasius, is justified both by their relation to the Council of Nicaea and by their place in history as having to do with the culmination of trends that are evident in the Ante-Nicene Fathers. Our attention to them will be largely confined to their significance for the development which preceded the Council of Nicaea. Their later activities (Athanasius did not die until almost fifty years after the Council of Nicaea was held) belong to the beginning of a new installment in church history rather than to the end of an old one. It is worthwhile to remember that they themselves were conscious of standing on such a boundary and of looking in both directions.

The Father of Church History

The fact that Eusebius was conscious of looking in both directions was due at least in part to his work as a historian. Repeatedly throughout this book we have had occasion to draw upon historical materials for which he is our only source. He himself was aware of being a pioneer in the field of church history. "We are," he said, "the first to undertake this present project and to attempt, as it were, to travel along a lonely and untrodden path." [1] Any scholar who attempts, as has been done in this volume, to trace the development of Christian institutions, literature, and thought during the second and third centuries must confess, as has one of the most eminent historians of that era, that "but for [Eusebius], we would know little about all this." [2]

It would be an amusing and instructive project to examine any of the standard modern histories of the early church with a view toward identifying how much of their total narrative content is in fact dependent on the *Ecclesiastical History* of Eusebius—the "father of church history."

In his zeal for documents Eusebius naturally also picked up a certain number of forgeries, most notably perhaps the legendary correspondence between Jesus and King Abgar of Edessa, in which Jesus promises to send one of his disciples to hear Abgar. The document seems to have originated near the end of the second century, but Eusebius accepted it as genuine.

Nevertheless, Eusebius does not deserve the reputation for naïve readiness to believe on uncertain evidence, a reputation he has acquired among some church historians. One has only to compare him either with his pagan predecessors and counterparts or with his Christian successors to recognize and admire the seriousness and honesty with which he did his research. In one respect, unfortunately, Eusebius resembles many other historians, past and present: his style is lacking in grace, and the *Ecclesiastical History* does not make very interesting reading. However, when Edward Gibbon asserts in *The Decline and Fall of the Roman Empire* that Eusebius "indirectly confesses that he has related whatever might redound [contribute] to the glory, and that he has suppressed all that could tend to the disgrace, of religion," [3] this is an accusation that will not stand up under critical scrutiny.

The Christianization of the Empire

The foregoing is not intended to mean that Eusebius was interested in historical objectivity in the modern sense—although it should be said that present-day historians are far less self-confident in making a claim to such objectivity than earlier generations of historians were. Eusebius had chosen sides in his narrative, and he knew which side ought to be (and would be) victorious; for as has been explained, his purpose was not only historical but apologetic. He wanted to prove that Christianity was not a novelty, but that it had an ancient and an honorable lineage. He also wanted to show that the Roman persecutors of the church were in error; and, like Augustine's *City of God* a century later, the *Ecclesiastical History* of Eusebius, especially in its last two books, is a celebration and a defense of the Christianization of the Roman Empire. The victory of Christianity meant not only peace for the church but even prosperity for the empire.

A comparison of the sentiments of Eusebius with some of the Christian otherworldliness described in previous chapters will reveal how radical a departure this represented from the attitudes of the earlier fathers. The *Epistle to Diognetus,* one of the writings of the apostolic fathers which we have not been able to consider in this book, declared:

> They [Christians] dwell in their own countries, but only as sojourn-
> ers; they bear their share in all things as citizens, and they endure all
> hardships as strangers. Every foreign country is a fatherland to them,
> and every fatherland is foreign.[4]

Such heroic sentiments were appropriate when Christians were a despised minority in the empire. They became even more fitting when the persecutions of the church became intense, as in the reign of emperors like Decius and Diocletian.

Now, however—in the time of Eusebius—the church had been granted toleration, and the Emperor Constantine had even become a Christian. Many of the earlier Christian attacks on the empire were suddenly outmoded. Of the Emperor Nero, Tertullian could say: "We glory in having our condemnation hallowed by the hostility of such a wretch."[5] However, when Eusebius quotes these words of Tertullian about a century later, he has to find other words

Does one come first? Eusebius reports that God appointed Constantine sovereign. Throughout Christian history, church members have agonized over the perplexities involved in the relation of church and state.

that will describe the relation of the church to the Roman Empire of Constantine.

Eusebius included such words not only in the closing sections of the *Ecclesiastical History*, but also in a special book, probably written between A.D. 337 and 340, on *The Life of Constantine*. Here Constantine is portrayed as "the first of all sovereigns who was regenerated and perfected [that is, baptized] in a church dedicated to the martyrs of Christ." [6] In a carefully written comparison of Constantine with his pagan predecessors on the imperial throne, Eusebius expressed his own conviction about the revolutionary change that had come about through this man: "Surely it must seem to all who duly regard these facts, that a new and fresh era of existence had begun to appear, and a light heretofore unknown suddenly to dawn from the midst of darkness on the human race: and all must confess that these things were entirely the work of God, who raised up this pious emperor to withstand the multitude of the ungodly." [7]

The historic significance of this change is almost impossible to exaggerate. In the Greek-speaking part of the empire, Constantine's empire continued at Constantinople, his new capital city, until the fall of that city to the Turks in 1453. In the West, the faltering authority of Constantinople over the old Romans and the new tribes gave way in A.D. 800 to the new supreme authority of Charlemagne. Charlemagne's domain eventually became known as "the holy Roman Empire," a reincarnation of the empire of Constantine that maintained some sort of existence from the coronation of Otto I in 962 until the formal end of the imperial succession, under pressure from Napoleon, in 1806.

At this time the medieval Western claim of succession from the Caesars and the pathetic spectacle of the late Hapsburg emperors were causing great turmoil. However, none of this should be permitted to take away from the stupendous fact that for more than a thousand years most of the Christian world was dominated by the idea of a Christian Roman Empire. Even today, the nostalgia of many Christians for "the good old days" of a Christian establishment and dominance over culture is an unknowing tribute to the work of Constantine, as celebrated by the father of church history—Eusebius.

112

Chapter Sixteen
ATHANASIUS

Orthodoxy in Alexandria

THE COUNCIL OF NICAEA in A.D. 325 is important not only in the history of the relations between Christianity and the state, but also in the history of Christian faith and doctrine. For it was at Nicaea that the church adopted the fundamental statement of its teaching which has come to be known, in a later revision, as the Nicene Creed.

The man whose name is inseparably linked with the Nicene Creed, even though he did not play a major role in its original formulation and adoption, is Athanasius (about 296–373). Through the bishop of Alexandria, Alexander, and through Athanasius, who succeeded Alexander in 328, the see of Alexandria, which had long been one of the most brilliant centers of piety and learning in all Christendom (see chapters eleven and twelve), likewise became the rallying point for Nicene orthodoxy. Or, to put the matter with stricter accuracy, the bishop of Alexandria became the rallying point, even when he was driven out of his city and forced into exile.

This happened to Athanasius five times in his career as bishop of Alexandria. He had been, in a real sense, born to be bishop. As a boy he had attracted the attention of Alexander and had been educated by the bishop. At the Council of Nicaea he served as an attendant to Alexander as what the Second Vatican Council has called a *peritus*, or theological consultant.

When Athanasius became bishop in A.D. 328, the creed adopted at Nicaea was the law in both church and state. However, the death of the Emperor Constantine brought on decades of political and theological conflict. With each change in the political atmosphere, the career of Athanasius underwent yet another shift. He was exiled

113

to Trier in A.D. 336 and to Rome in 339, driven into exiles nearer home in 356 and again in 363, and sent into a final exile in 365. He returned to assume his rightful place as bishop of Alexandria each time; and he was at least permitted to die there, on May 2, 373.

The doctrines of Nicaea and of Athanasius will be discussed shortly, but at least something should be said here of Athanasius' character. Edward Gibbon, whose negative comments on Eusebius we have quoted in chapter fifteen, was obliged to pay Athanasius this grudging tribute:

> Amid the storms of persecution, the archbishop of Alexandria was patient of labor, jealous of fame, careless of safety; and although his mind was tainted by the contagion of fanaticism, Athanasius displayed a superiority of character and abilities which would have qualified him, far better than the degenerate sons of Constantine, for the government of a great monarchy.[1]

A group of orthodox Christians fleeing in a boat set afire by the Arians.

Throughout a turbulent life Athanasius retained a courage and a serenity that enabled him to defend what he believed to be the essential truth of the Christian gospel without losing himself in controversial arguments. His language is often harsh. Yet behind it is not a self-seeking church dignitary who identified his vanity with the glory of God, but an obedient theologian who would not yield his convictions to political or personal pressure.

The Doctrine of the Trinity

It is, of course, impossible to summarize the Christian doctrine of the Trinity in a few pages of such a book as this. Nevertheless, if the struggle over the Arian heresy was, as Cardinal Newman said, a defense against those who assumed that there could not be any mystery in the doctrine of the Scriptures in regard to the nature of God, no study of the fathers of the early church is complete

Arians setting fire to an orthodox Christian church.

without at least some account of the doctrinal and, indeed, creedal outcome of their reflections and speculations on the relation of Jesus Christ to God the Father. That outcome was the doctrine of the Trinity, as summarized in the confession of faith eventually known as the Nicene Creed:

> I believe in one God, the Father Almighty, Maker of heaven and earth and of all things visible and invisible. And in one Lord Jesus Christ, the only-begotten Son of God, begotten of the Father before all ages, God of God, Light of Light, very God of very God, begotten not made, being of one substance with the Father, through whom all things were made: who for us men and for our salvation came down from heaven, was incarnate by the Holy Spirit of the Virgin Mary, and was made man: who for us, too, was crucified under Pontius Pilate, suffered, and was buried: the third day he rose according to the Scriptures, ascended into heaven, and is seated on the right hand of the Father: he shall come again with glory to judge the living and the dead, and his kingdom shall have no end. And in the Holy Spirit, the Lord and Giver of life, who proceeds from the Father and the Son: who together with the Father and the Son is worshiped and glorified: who spoke by the prophets. And I believe in one holy Catholic and apostolic church. I acknowledge one baptism for the remission of sins, and I look for the resurrection of the dead and the life of the age to come. Amen.

Almost every phrase of this statement of faith has been debated and reinterpreted during the past fifteen centuries, as theologians have sought to define the relation between their thought and the affirmations of the creed. It is really not very difficult to find a great difference between these affirmations and anything that the Christians of the twentieth century feel able to declare. It is, however, much harder to improvise any other statement of faith which will say everything that the Nicene Creed says without saying anything that the modern Christian does not feel able to say. The statements of faith put together by the denominations of the twentieth century may be more honest in some ways, but to many readers they are certainly no more convincing than the hoary creeds of the Greek fathers. For to be Christian means, as an irreducible minimum, to affirm that what happened in the life, death, and resurrection of Jesus Christ is a deed of which no one but God was capable, and that consequently there is a unique connection between Jesus of Nazareth and the One by whom all things exist and live.

Portraits of Christ in early centuries.

A contemporary portrait of Christ.

Once anyone has said this much—as everyone entitled to the name "Christian" probably has to say—it is only a step, even though an extremely long step, to some sort of doctrine of the Trinity. For, in the words of a distinguished modern scholar whom no one can justly accuse of sentimental traditionalism:

> The perennial meaning of the doctrine of the Trinity is . . . the expo sition of the Christian doctrine of God in so far as it rests in the experience of God's revelation in Jesus. It expounds the immanent actuality of the transcendent meaning of life in history and in human experience on the basis of the presupposition that God is knowable only through Jesus the Christ.[2]

This presupposition is shared by most Christians, even by those who find the traditional formulations of the doctrine of the Trinity unacceptable. The central issue in the controversy over the Trinity was whether the Son of God, who appeared upon the earth and reunited men with God, was identical with the highest divine Being who rules in heaven and earth, or whether he was a demigod. Or, in the words of Athanasius, "Who is there in all mankind . . . who ventures to rank among creatures One whom he confesses the while to be God?"[3]

Thus the issues which we have examined throughout this brief study—the apostolic character of the church, the meaning of the Christian witness, the nature of Christian discipline, the authority of apostolic revelation, the relation of Christianity and Judaism, the definition of the church as a community that includes both sinners and intellectuals in its fellowship, the problem of the interpretation of Holy Scripture versus speculation, and the emergence of fixed forms in the church—are all expressed in the doctrine of the Trinity, where each of them is either restated or rendered quite irrelevant. In our efforts to design relevant formulations and reformulations of the doctrine, therefore, the lives and works of the fathers of the early church are a major resource. While we cannot make their answers our answers, it is impossible for us to evade making their questions our questions.

Acknowledgments

INTRODUCTION
1. From *Annales* by Tacitus (xv, 44).

CHAPTER TWO
1. From *I Clement* (46, 9).*
2. From *Ecclesiastical History* by Eusebius (III, 16).

CHAPTER THREE
1. From *St. Ignatius and Christianity in Antioch* by Virginia Corwin. Yale University Press, New Haven, 1960 (p. 30). Used by permission.
2. From *Epistle to the Romans* by Ignatius (4, 1).*
3. From *Epistle to the Magnesians* by Ignatius (10, 3; 13, 1).*
4. From *Epistle to the Romans* by Ignatius (2, 2).*
5. From *Epistle to the Smyrneans* by Ignatius (5, 2).*
6. *Ibid.* (8, 2).*

CHAPTER FOUR
1. From *Against Heresies* by Irenaeus (III, 3, 4).
2. From *The Martyrdom of Polycarp* (3).
3. *Ibid.* (6, 2).
4. *Ibid.* (9, 3).
5. *Ibid.* (14, 2).

CHAPTER FIVE
1. From "Letters (Latin)" by Robert Graham Cochrane Levens in *The Oxford Classical Dictionary*, ed. by M. Cary et al. Oxford University Press, London, 1949 (p. 497).
2. From *The Shepherd* by Hermas (Visions II, 2, 5).
3. *Ibid.* (Mandates I, 1).
4. *Ibid.* (Mandates IX, 6).
5. *Ibid.* (Similitudes v, 3, 5–6).
6. *Ibid.* (Similitudes x, 4, 4).

Chapter Six

1. From *An Introduction to New Testament Thought* by Frederick C. Grant. Abingdon Press, Nashville, 1950 (p. 30).
2. From *Gnosticism:* A Sourcebook of Heretical Writings from the Early Christian Period, ed. by Robert M. Grant. Harper and Row, Publishers, New York, 1961 (p. 18).
3. Translated from *Marcion:* Das Evangelium vom fremdon Gott, Vol. I, by Adolf Harnack. Leipzig, 2nd edition 1924 (p. 154).
4. *Ibid.* (ii, 256).

Chapter Seven

1. From *Against Heresies* by Irenaeus (iii, 4, 3).
2. From *Against the Valentinians* by Tertullian (iv).
3. From *Against Heresies* by Irenaeus (i, 5, 3).
4. *Ibid.* (i, 6, 1).
5. *Ibid.* (v, 9; i, 6, 2).
6. *Ibid.* (i, 7, 2).
7. *Ibid.* (i, 6, 2).

Chapter Eight

1. From *Ecclesiastical History* by Eusebius (iv, 3, 1).
2. From *The Founding of the Church Universal* by Hans Lietzmann (trans. by Bertram Lee Woolf). Lutterworth Press, London, and World Publishing Company, New York, 1958 (p. 185). Used by permission.
3. From *Dialogue with Trypho* by Justin (2).
4. *Ibid.* (8).
5. From *Ecclesiastical History* by Eusebius (iv, 11, 8).
6. From *Apology* by Justin (i, 6).
7. *Ibid.* (i, 23).
8. *Ibid.* (i, 12).
9. From *Adversus Judaeos:* A Bird's Eye View of Christian *Apologiae* until the Renaissance by A. Lukyn Williams. Cambridge University Press, London, 1935 (p. 18).
10. From *Dialogue with Trypho* by Justin (55).
11. From *Dialogue with Trypho* by Justin (125, 135).

Chapter Nine

1. From *St. Irenaeus:* Proof of the Apostolic Preaching, ed. by Joseph P. Smith, S.J. (*Ancient Christian Writers*, Vol. XVI). Newman Press, Westminster, Md., 1952 (pp. 43–44).*
2. From *Ecclesiastical History* by Eusebius (v, 24, 18).
3. From *Against Heresies* by Irenaeus (i, 10, 1).
4. *Ibid.* (iii, 4, 1).
5. *Ibid.* (iii, 1, 1).

6. *Ibid.* (III, 3, 1).
7. *Ibid.* (III, 3, 2).
8. *Ibid.* (III, 5, 1).
9. *Ibid.* (v, 27, 2).
10. *Ibid.* (IV, 6, 6).
11. From *Proof of the Apostolic Preaching* by Irenaeus (31).*
12. From *Against Heresies* by Irenaeus (II, 22, 4).

CHAPTER TEN

1. From *Christian Morals Today* by John A. T. Robinson. Copyright © SCM Press, Ltd. 1964 and published 1964 U. S. A. by The Westminster Press. (pp. 12–13). Used by permission.
2. From "De Spect. 30" quoted in *Christianity and Classical Culture: A Study of Thought and Action from Augustus to Augustine* by Charles Norris Cochrane. Oxford University Press, New York and London, 1944 (p. 230).
3. From *Patrology*, Vol. II, by Johannes Quasten. Newman Press, Westminster, Md., 1953 (p. 247).
4. From *Ecclesiastical History* by Eusebius (v, 16, 7).
5. From *On the Soul* by Tertullian (55).
6. From *On Penitence* by Tertullian (7).*
7. From *On the Good of Widowhood* by Augustine (6).
8. From *To His Wife* by Tertullian (1, 1).*
9. *Ibid.* (2, 8).*
10. From *An Exhortation to Chastity* by Tertullian (9).*
11. From *Enthusiasm: A Chapter in the History of Religion* by Ronald Knox. Oxford University Press, New York, 1961 (p. 49).
12. From *On Fasting* by Tertullian (1).
13. From *Concerning Flight in Persecution* by Tertullian (11).
14. From *On Purity* by Tertullian (16).
15. *Ibid.* (21).

CHAPTER ELEVEN

1. From *Ecclesiastical History* by Eusebius (v, 10, 1).
2. From *Stromateis* by Clement of Alexandria (I, 1).
3. From *Ecclesiastical History* by Eusebius (VI, 3, 3).
4. *Ibid.* (VI, 11, 6).
5. From *Stromateis* by Clement of Alexandria (I, 1).
6. From *History of Dogma*, Vol. II, by Adolf Harnack (trans. by Neil Buchanan). Dover Publications, New York, 1961 (p. 324).

CHAPTER TWELVE

1. From *Ecclesiastical History* by Eusebius (VI, 2, 2).
2. *Ibid.* (VI, 2, 10).
3. From *The Founding of the Church Universal* by Hans Lietzman (p. 316). Used by permission.

4. From *Panegyric on Origen* by Gregory the Wonder-Worker (15).
5. From *The Song of Songs* by Origen (I, 3).*
6. *Ibid.* (III, 12).*
7. From *Homilies on Joshua* by Origen (XXI, 1).
8. From *Fathers and Heretics* by G. L. Prestige. S.P.C.K., London, 1948 (p. 54).
9. From *Origen:* Contra Celsum, ed. by Henry Chadwick. Cambridge University Press, London, 1953 (p. ix).
10. From *Homilies on Luke* by Origen (XVI, 6).
11. From *Allegory and Event* by Richard P. C. Hanson. John Knox Press, Richmond, 1959 (p. 354).

CHAPTER THIRTEEN

1. From *Ecclesiastical History* by Eusebius (VI, 20, 3).
2. From *On Illustrious Men* by Jerome (61).
3. From *The Treatise on the Apostolic Tradition of St. Hippolytus of Rome*, ed. by Gregory Dix. S.P.C.K., London, 1937 (Introduction). Used by permission.
4. *Ibid.* (p. 4).
5. *Ibid.* (p. 23).

CHAPTER FOURTEEN

1. From *Where We Are in Church Union*, ed. by George L. Hunt and Paul A. Crow, Jr. A Reflection Book, Association Press, New York, 1965 (p. 92). Used by permission.
2. *Ibid.* (p. 93).
3. From *Epistle XIV* by Cyprian (1).
4. From *Life* by Pontius (19).
5. From *The Unity of the Catholic Church* by Cyprian (7).*
6. From *The Lapsed* by Cyprian (16).*
7. From *Epistle LI* by Cyprian (24).
8. From *The Unity of the Catholic Church* by Cyprian (8).*
9. From *Epistle LXVIII* by Cyprian (8).
10. From *The Donatist Church:* A Movement of Protest in Roman North Africa by W. H. C. Frend. Oxford University Press, London, 1952 (p. 140).
11. From *Epistle LXXI* by Cyprian (1).*

CHAPTER FIFTEEN

1. From *Ecclesiastical History* by Eusebius (I, 1, 3).
2. From *The Early Christian Church*, Vol. II, by Philip Carrington. Cambridge University Press, London, 1957 (p. 475).
3. From *The Decline and Fall of the Roman Empire* by Edward Gibbon. (chapter 16).
4. From *Epistle to Diognetus* (5, 5).*

5. From *Apology* by Tertullian (5).
6. From *Life of Constantine* by Eusebius (III, 52).
7. *Ibid.* (III, 1).

CHAPTER SIXTEEN

1. From *The Decline and Fall of the Roman Empire* by Edward Gibbon.
2. From *The Heritage of the Reformation* by Wilhelm Pauck. The Free Press, New York, 1961 (2nd edition) (p. 191). Used by permission.
3. From *Orations Against the Arians* by Athanasius (I, 3).

* From *Ancient Christian Writers*, ed. by Joseph P. Smith, S. J. The Newman Press, Westminster, Md., and Longmans, Green & Company, Essex. Used by permission of the publishers.